THE CHRONICLES OF

NARNIA

WARDROBE

...ide to Narnia

LINCOLNSHIRE COUNTY COUNCIL
EDUCATION AND CULTURAL SERVICES.
This book should be returned on or before
the last date shown below.

NB3

BRANSTON
2 3 MAR 2007
Tel: 01522 791323

14. JUN 11.
C JUL 2011

17. MAY 06

KIRTON
25 JUL 2011

SEP 2007

Waddington Library
- - SEP 2006
01522 720346

16. JAN 12

28. MAR 08
MC2 Ruskington Library
01522 782010

23. OCT 06.
26.   07.
23. AUG

28. MAR. 09

To renew or order library books visit
www.lincolnshire.gov.uk
You will require a Personal Identification Number.
Ask any member of staff for this

KIRK

Beyond the wardrobe : the official guide

£12.99   J823.912   JNF

L 5/9

by E. J. Kirk

Based on *The Chronicles of Narnia* by C. S. Lewis

HarperCollins*Publishers*

AD 04081502

LINCOLNSHIRE COUNTY COUNCIL	
04081502	
PETERS	£12.99
28-Feb-06	J823.912

HarperCollins*Publishers*

77-85 Fulham Palace Road, London W6 8JB

www.harpercollins.co.uk

Published by HarperCollins*Publishers* 2005

1

Copyright © 2005 by C.S. Lewis Pte Ltd

www.narnia.com

The Chronicles of Narnia®, Narnia® and all book titles, characters and locales original to The Chronicles of Narnia
are trademarks of C.S. Lewis Pte. Ltd. Use without permission is strictly prohibited.

Quotes from *The Chronicles of Narnia* by C.S. Lewis; copyright © 1950, 1951,
1952, 1953, 1954, 1955, 1956 by C.S. Lewis Pte. Ltd. Used by permission.
Conceptual artwork and still images from *The Chronicles of Narnia: The Lion, the Witch and the Wardrobe* film
copyright © 2005 Disney Enterprises, Inc. and Walden Media, LLC.
Artwork by Pauline Baynes; copyright © 1998 by C.S. Lewis Pte. Ltd.
Artwork by Tudor Humphries; copyright © 2004 by C.S. Lewis Pte. Ltd.
Artwork by Cliff Nielsen; copyright © 2001 by C.S. Lewis Pte. Ltd.

ISBN 0 00 720571 6

Printed in Italy

This book is sold subject to the condition that it shall not, by way of trade or otherwise,
be lent, re-sold, hired out or otherwise circulated without the publisher's prior consent in
any form of binding or cover other than that in which it is published and without a similar
condition including this condition being imposed on the subsequent purchaser.

All rights reserved. No part of this publication may be reproduced, stored in a retrieval system,
or transmitted, in any form or by any means, electronic, mechanical, photocopying, recording
or otherwise, without the prior permission of the publishers.

Contents

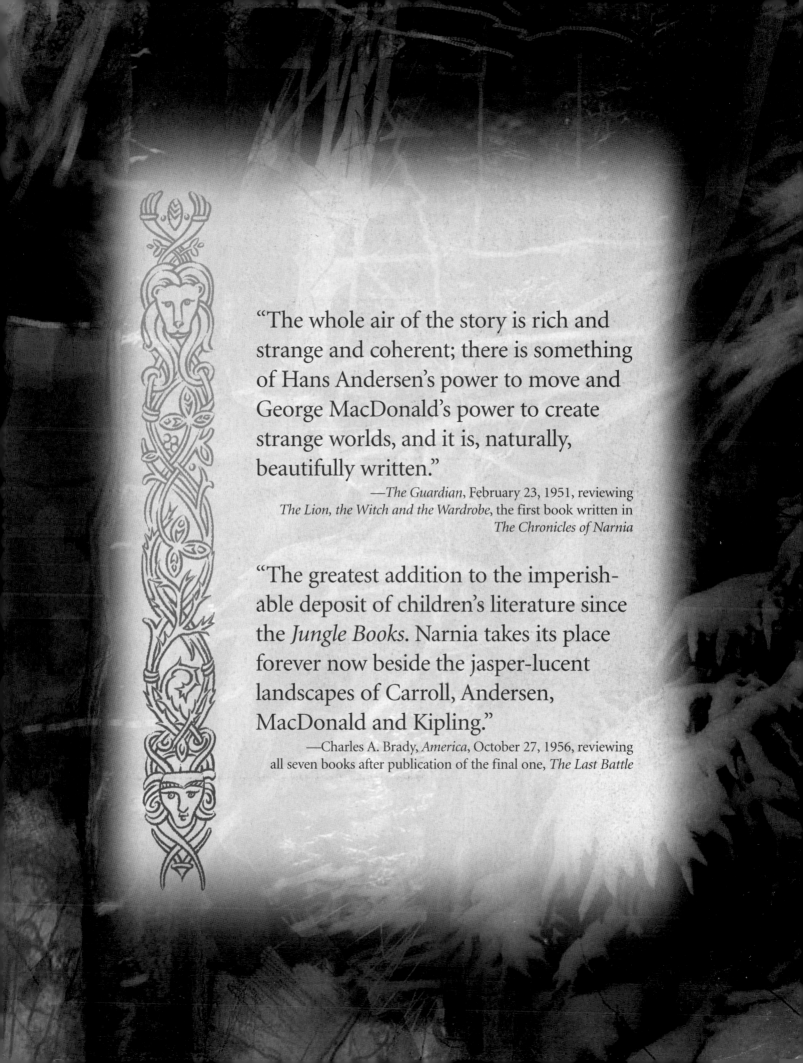

"The whole air of the story is rich and strange and coherent; there is something of Hans Andersen's power to move and George MacDonald's power to create strange worlds, and it is, naturally, beautifully written."

—*The Guardian*, February 23, 1951, reviewing
The Lion, the Witch and the Wardrobe, the first book written in
The Chronicles of Narnia

"The greatest addition to the imperishable deposit of children's literature since the *Jungle Books*. Narnia takes its place forever now beside the jasper-lucent landscapes of Carroll, Andersen, MacDonald and Kipling."

—Charles A. Brady, *America*, October 27, 1956, reviewing
all seven books after publication of the final one, *The Last Battle*

Entering the Wardrobe

Narnia. "It is the country of Aslan, the country of the Waking Trees and Visible Naiads, of Fauns and Satyrs, of Dwarfs and Giants, of the gods and the Centaurs, of Talking Beasts." That is how author and scholar C. S. Lewis had Doctor Cornelius, a wise old half-Dwarf and beloved tutor, describe Narnia in the book PRINCE CASPIAN. Doctor Cornelius is describing a land that has become one of the most important fictional places ever imagined. More than fifty years since its invention in THE LION, THE WITCH AND

In the movie The Lion, the Witch and the Wardrobe, *Lewis's original vision of a Faun is faithfully represented.*

In 1948, decades after his first conception of Narnia, Lewis wrote The Lion, the Witch and the Wardrobe, *describing Lucy Pevensie's trip through the wardrobe and the magical world she found there.*

the Wardrobe, Narnia has enchanted the hearts and minds of generations around the globe. First published in the 1950s, *The Chronicles of Narnia* have remained the benchmark for literary fantasy. To discover how and why the seven books have worked their magic on readers and achieved their special place in literature will require looking, to borrow one of Lewis's images, on all sides of the wardrobe—at the life of the author and deep inside the world he created. Because *The Chronicles of Narnia* originate in C. S. Lewis's life—his experiences, sense of humour, deep interests, hobbies, loves, fears and dreams.

Narnia first began to take form when Lewis was just sixteen years old. An image popped into his mind of a Faun—a mythical creature with the head and chest of a man and the legs of a goat—carrying an umbrella and parcels in a snowy wood. Decades later, in his late forties, he began the serious work of imagining the rest of Narnia. By that time (the late 1940s), Lewis was already famous for having written many books for adults. But as a lifelong lover of fantasy and mythology, he believed that fairy tales and myths are sometimes the best way to say what needs to be said. And Lewis still had a great deal to say.

Traditionally fairy tales are about ordinary people, usually children, who overcome great hardships to do extraordinary things. There are often long, arduous journeys and fierce confrontations before the happy endings are achieved. Lewis believed that after reading fantasy, the reader returns to the real world with renewed pleasure, awe and satisfaction. The boy "does not despise real woods because he has read of enchanted woods: the reading makes all real woods a little enchanted."

Lewis was sceptical at first about whether he could write about children, claiming to be ill at ease around them. But it helped that he remembered his own childhood very well. He finally put pen to paper and then read the first few pages to his trusted friend and former pupil Roger Lancelyn Green, who was himself a writer of children's books. Spurred on by his friend's excitement and encouragement, Lewis at last allowed himself to transfer the decades-old image of the faun from his head onto the page and into Narnia.

Through the tales of Narnia, Lewis swept readers into a magical world. But his purpose was not simply to divert readers

First Impressions

Roger Lancelyn Green was the first to hear passages from what would become *The Lion, the Witch and the Wardrobe*. He said of the experience, "As [Lewis] read, there had crept over me a feeling of awe and excitement: not only that it was better than most children's books which were appearing at the time—but the conviction that I was listening to the first reading of a great classic."

Lewis himself wrote, "... I am not quite sure what made me, In a particular year of my life, feel that not only a fairy tale, but a fairy tale addressed to children, was exactly what I must write—or burst. Partly, I think, that this form permits, or compels you to leave out things I wanted to leave out. It compels you to throw all the force of the book into what was done and said."

Decades later, in 1990, literary critic Phoebe Pettingell had this to say: "Once [Lewis] finally recognized that...he was primarily a storyteller, he composed *The Chronicles of Narnia* to recreate the atmosphere of 'joy' that animated his youth. The seven enchanting fantasies capture a child's wonder in a world where marvellous possibilities seem to lurk around every corner....[and support Lewis's] critical insight that literature helps us mythologize our lives."

with fantasy. Rather, Lewis wanted to return his readers to reality equipped with new images and metaphors that would help them find magic in their own lives. He used fantasy to present his audience with ways to handle reality bravely and honestly. His young heroes faced powerful enemies but none more daunting than their own human failings. To succeed at their heroic tasks, they were forced to confront both the worst of evil creatures and the worst in themselves.

Lewis's central interest was the endless war between good and evil and the myriad ways, from the ordinary to the heroic, in which individuals become involved in the battle. It is a struggle that engages every human being. Twice in Lewis's lifetime, this struggle also had enveloped him, his nation and whole continents in the two world wars. Lewis initially conjured three powerful images for his representation of this epic struggle: the Lion, the Witch and the wardrobe.

The Lion, Lewis's golden-maned metaphor for the power of goodness, simply leapt into the world of Narnia fully formed, joining the Faun in the snowy landscape that Lewis had first seen in his teens. "[S]uddenly Aslan came bounding into it," Lewis wrote, recalling the moment in his forties when the image of the Great Lion first occurred to him. "I think I had been having a good many dreams of lions about that time. Apart from that, I don't know where the Lion came from or why He came. But once He was there He pulled the whole story together, and soon He pulled the six other Narnian stories in after Him."

One of Lewis's favourite books might have influenced the character of Aslan. *The Place of the Lion*, by fantasy writer Charles Williams, was a work of classical philosophy cloaked as a fantasy novel. After reading the book in 1936, Lewis introduced himself to Williams in a letter, writing, "I have just read your *Place of the Lion* and it is to me one of the major literary events of my life. . . ." The pair became close friends.

Lewis's choice for the incarnation of evil speaks to his education as a classical scholar. "The Witch is of course Circe," he wrote on July 30, 1954, in a letter to William Kinter, an American. Lewis was referring to the sorceress in Homer's *Odyssey* who greeted men as welcome guests to her island and then magically turned them into animals. "[S]he is…the same Archetype we find in so many fairy tales. No good asking where any individual author got *that*. We are born knowing the Witch, aren't we?"

The final image in this triptych, the wardrobe, comes from Lewis's childhood. It takes its place as one of literature's most enduring metaphors for the magical connection between common reality and the most idealistic dreams. Lewis recognized

GOOD
and...

"Suddenly Aslan came bounding into it," Lewis wrote of the moment he first imagined the Great Lion. Aslan became his golden-maned metaphor for the power of goodness in the eternal struggle against evil.

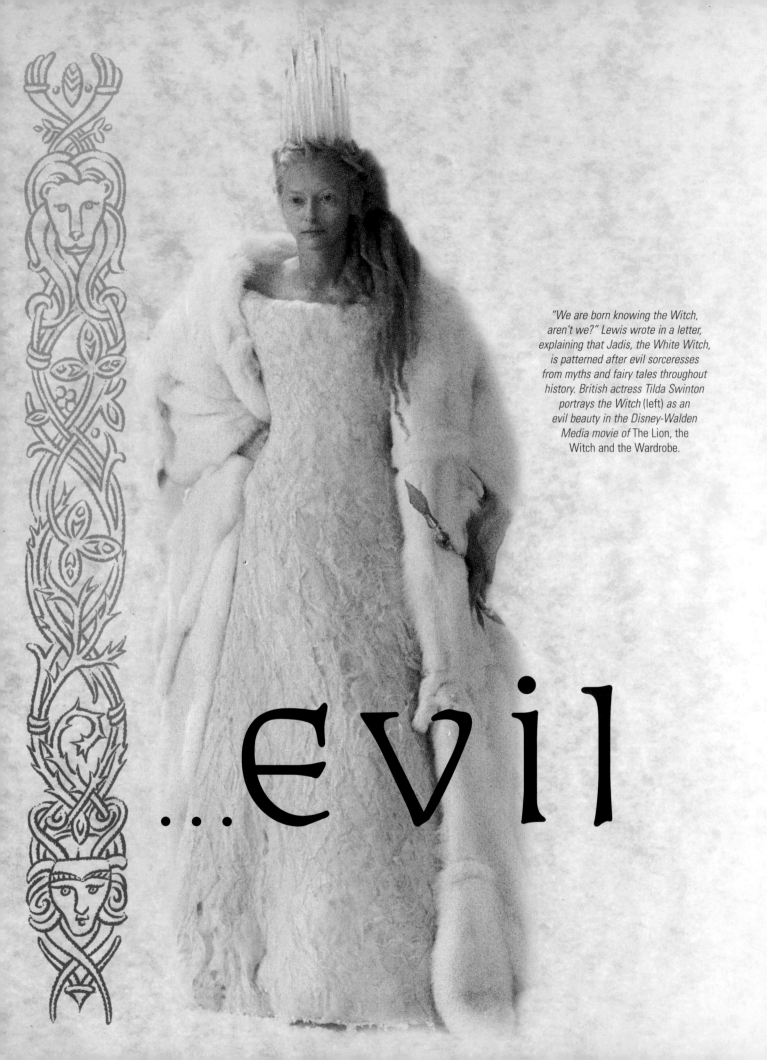

"We are born knowing the Witch, aren't we?" Lewis wrote in a letter, explaining that Jadis, the White Witch, is patterned after evil sorceresses from myths and fairy tales throughout history. British actress Tilda Swinton portrays the Witch (left) as an evil beauty in the Disney-Walden Media movie of The Lion, the Witch and the Wardrobe.

...evil

that most people live day by day without ever feeling engaged in the great issues of existence. So Lewis provided the wardrobe, a fantasy bridge that leads each reader directly to the front lines of the greatest struggle there is: the battle for goodness against evil.

Though unfamiliar to many contemporary youths, wardrobes were common in Lewis's day. While he made it clear that there was no specific wardrobe that inspired the one that led to Narnia in *The Lion, the Witch and the Wardrobe*, his family, no doubt, owned several, including a large oak one that his grandfather built.

As rich and fascinating as the Lion, the Witch and the wardrobe are, there is far more to Narnia: the Talking Animals that fill *The Chronicles*; the great ships and sea creatures; the brave heroes and treacherous villains; and the landscape of the Narnian world itself, with its high mountain peaks, white-capped seas and windblown deserts.

The way to trace the origins of Narnia is to start at the beginning, in 1898, when C. S. Lewis was born in Ireland, a land that is, itself, no stranger to magical tales, fantastic characters and otherworldly landscapes.

Pieces of Narnia in Illinois

A wardrobe that belonged to the Lewis family is now in the Marion E. Wade Center at Wheaton College in Wheaton, Illinois, where anyone can visit it. Lewis's writing desk and a vast collection of personal letters and other memorabilia, such as a pen, pipe and a well-worn tea mug, are also there. The Wade Center houses memorabilia from many of Lewis's friends and contemporaries as well.

The wardrobe is seven feet tall and four feet wide and is filled with period-style coats, including one that belonged to Lewis's brother, Warren. There is a sign on the wardrobe door: "Enter at your own risk. The Wade Center assumes no responsibility for persons who disappear or who are lost in this wardrobe."

The Tale-Teller's Secrets

—

Born in Belfast, Ireland, on November 29, 1898, Clive Staples Lewis never liked his name. So when he was four, he decided to change it. He marched up to his mother and pointed to his chest and announced his name would be "Jacksie". As he grew up, it became "Jack", and that was how he was known to his friends for the rest of his life. Lewis also invented his older brother's nickname, Warnie. Warren was three years older, and the two were very close.

The lush Irish countryside in which he was reared agreed with Lewis more than the name he was given. By the age of four, Clive Staples Lewis (as an infant, above) had dubbed himself "Jacksie"— and Jack he was from then on.

Little Lea still stands today (main photo) *at 76 Circular Road, Strandtown, Belfast, looking much as it did from 1905 to 1930* (inset) *when the Lewis family lived there. Lewis wrote that the house was "almost a major character in my story".*

Lewis's father, Albert, was a solicitor in the local police court, but he enjoyed writing poetry and telling stories. Lewis's mother, Flora, the daughter of an Anglican rector, studied to be a mathematician. Recalling his parents in one of his books, *Surprised by Joy*, Lewis described his father's side of the family as "true Welshmen, sentimental, passionate, and rhetorical, easily moved both to anger and to tenderness; men who laughed and cried a great deal. . . ." His mother's family, on the other hand, he called "a cooler race. Their minds were critical and ironic. . . ." Interestingly, Lewis concluded that his mercurial and emotional paternal relatives "had not much of the talent for happiness", while his mother's more logical family had that talent "in a high degree".

His parents' house was filled with books, and they passed their love of literature to their sons. Young Jack's favourite books included *Treasure Island, Gulliver's Travels*, and any book by E. Nesbit or Beatrix Potter. When he got a little older, he loved to read novels by H. G. Wells and Mark Twain, as well as Sir Arthur Conan Doyle's Sherlock Holmes mysteries.

Rain was a seemingly interminable feature of the Irish climate. In addition, there was the real threat of tuberculosis, which was epidemic throughout Europe for decades and, until the development of antibiotics in the 1940s, was treated mainly by isolating the sick from the healthy. These factors combined to keep the Lewis brothers indoors much of the time. The boys had a nanny who loved Ireland's folk legends and fairy tales about leprechauns, saints and monsters. As the boys sat and listened to her stories on rainy afternoons, Lewis's lifelong love of folklore was born. Jack's relationship to his nanny may have been

the inspiration for the nurse in *Prince Caspian*, who taught Caspian the true history of Narnia.

When Lewis was seven, his family moved to a new house in the country, on the outskirts of Belfast. Keeping with the British tradition of giving names even to rather ordinary homes, the Lewis house was called Little Lea. It was much bigger than their previous house in the city and had a lot of spare rooms. Lewis and Warnie spent hours in the attic creating their own fantasy worlds. They made up the complete history of an imaginary world that they named Boxen.

Of the move to the country, Lewis would later write, "The New House is almost a

As an adult, Lewis loved to take his walking stick and trek through the countryside (right). Three generations posed around 1900 for this Lewis family portrait (above). Jack is the infant seated on his aunt Agnes's lap (far right). His mother, Flora (far left), holds his brother, Warnie. His father, Albert, stands next to Jack's grandmother. His grandfather is seated (centre).

major character in my story. I am a product of long corridors, empty sunlit rooms, upstairs indoor silences, attics explored in solitude, distant noises of gurgling cisterns and pipes, and the noise of wind under the tiles."

When the weather cooperated, the brothers loved to ride their bikes through the countryside and explore. They also enjoyed watching the boats leave from Belfast's harbour, which they could see in the distance from their house. They imagined the sailors' adventures and hoped to one day have their own.

When Jack was nine, his mother became very ill. She died of cancer a few months later, leaving the family devastated. Many years later, Lewis returned to this painful period when he wrote in *The Magician's Nephew* about a boy whose mother is dying.

Jack Lewis's formal education began after his mother's death, and his experiences at school were almost uniformly bad. The difficulties he encountered made him a lifelong critic of British schooling in general and boarding schools in particular. Still, his deep dislike for schools was surpassed by his deeper love of learning and knowledge. His ability to separate schooling from learning influenced the pages of *The Chronicles* and marked the independent intellectual course of his life.

Lewis's worst school experience by far was his first: Wynyard House, a poorly run boarding school in Hertfordshire, where Warnie was already a student. Both Lewis boys were miserable there. Wynyard was eventually shut by the courts.

Jack navigated his way through four schools, finding solace in both ideas and close friends, which would prove to be the stable centres of a lifetime. Ideas he found in abundance in the school libraries. His other anchor was corresponding with his friend Arthur Greeves, who lived across the street from Little Lea. Arthur shared Lewis's love of mythology and legends. The two remained close for the rest of their lives.

Lewis finally found the intellectual mentor he had always wanted when he was sent to England at the age of fifteen to be privately tutored by an old teacher of his father's, W. T. Kirkpatrick. Under his guidance, Lewis became the scholar he had always wanted to be. He learned foreign languages easily, studied classical literature, and was

After moving to Little Lea when Jack was seven, the Lewis boys (opposite page) *explored hill and dale on their bicycles whenever the weather allowed. Jack Lewis remained close to his older brother, Warnie* (on the right)*, throughout his life.*

In 1930, Lewis first saw The Kilns (inset below)*, which took its name from the conical brick kilns in the middle of the grounds. The estate where he would live the rest of his life is preserved today as a study centre* (main photo below)*.*

taught how to present his thoughts clearly. So it is no surprise that when Jack wrote *The Lion, the Witch and the Wardrobe*, the character who offers the best advice to the children is ageing Professor Kirke, named in honour of Lewis's beloved tutor. (While the name "Kirke" doesn't appear in *The Lion, the Witch and the Wardrobe*, it is clear that the Professor is Digory Kirke, the boy hero of *The Magician's Nephew*, all grown up.)

Lewis's hard work with Professor Kirkpatrick paid off, and he was accepted to study at Oxford University. This was

Moore. When Jack and Paddy were still in the Officer Training Corps in Oxford, they made a pact to take care of each other's family if one of them didn't survive. When their training was complete, the two new second lieutenants were assigned to different outfits; Moore was sent to the Rifle Brigade, while Lewis served with the Somerset Light Infantry.

After Paddy was killed in 1918, Lewis kept up his end of the agreement: he took care of Paddy's mother for the rest of her life. Wounded in three places, Lewis was sent

"My external surroundings are beautiful beyond expectation...."

Lewis's dream come true, and he thought he had never seen a place as beautiful. He wasn't there for long though, before World War I changed his life. In 1917, Lewis enlisted in the army, underwent officers' training at Oxford and was sent into battle in France.

The war was brutal, and Lewis saw many of his friends killed. His closest friend was another Irishman named Edward "Paddy"

back to England to recuperate in a hospital. Although he would always have shrapnel embedded in his chest, Lewis was eventually able to return to college.

Paddy Moore's mother and her daughter, Maureen, lived near Oxford, and with them, Lewis had a semblance of family life. Jack excelled academically and published a book of poetry called *Spirits in Bondage*. As his undergraduate years came to a close,

BOXEN

Warnie loved making tiny models, one of which, a miniature garden, filled Jack with a particular sense of joy and wonder. To create his own fantasy worlds, Jack turned to writing.

Lewis wrote, "Here [in the attic room] my first stories were written, and illustrated, with enormous satisfaction. They were an attempt to combine my two chief literary pleasures—'dressed animals' and 'knights in armour'. As a result, I wrote about chivalrous mice and rabbits who rode out in complete mail to kill not giants but cats."

The hero of the Boxen stories was a brave mouse named Peter who lived in a medieval country called Animal-Land, where animals dressed in fine clothes and spoke like people. Lewis created a history of Animal-Land that dated back seven hundred years, and he drew pictures of the main characters along with detailed illustrations of ships and maps of the land.

Little did Lewis realize that more than forty years later he would once again write about talking animals dressed in fine clothes. He kept the name Peter for the eldest child, who eventually is crowned High King of Narnia in *The Lion, the Witch and the Wardrobe*. The brave mouse grew up to be Reepicheep, who was featured in *Prince Caspian* and *The Voyage of the* Dawn Treader. Although Animal-Land was clearly good practice for what would come later in his writing life, Lewis insisted that it and Narnia were two very different places "except [for] the anthropomorphic beasts. Animal-Land, by its whole quality, excluded the least hint of wonder. . . . [T]here was no poetry, even no romance, in it."

Narnia's Reepicheep (right), *the brave mouse, was not the first valiant talking animal Lewis imagined. As a boy, he created "Boxen" stories and drawings, including this 1910 watercolour* (above) *of "the lobby of the house".*

to his heart and mind, he decided to accept a short-term position teaching philosophy at Oxford's University College.

Lewis flourished in his first appointment, and in 1925, he took on the job that he would keep for the next thirty years: a tutor and lecturer in the English department of Oxford's Magdalen College. As was the tradition, he was given a suite of rooms to live in on campus. In a letter to his father, Lewis wrote, "My external surroundings are beautiful beyond expectation and beyond hope."

In 1929, Lewis's father passed away. Lewis had been able to spend some time with him during the year before his death, and he was grateful for that. But Warnie had been in China when their father died. A few months later, after Warnie's return, the brothers went back to Little Lea one last time and ceremoniously buried their Boxen toys in the garden.

LEWIS'S READING LIST

George MacDonald *(Phantastes)*

Homer *(The Iliad* and *The Odyssey)*

Plato

Malory *(Le Morte d'Arthur)*

Norse myths (Siegfried and the Twilight of the Gods), Celtic, Greek and Arabian myths

---

Lewis had to make a decision about his future. It was clear to Jack that happiness for him was the life of the intellectual.

Ordinary pursuits like law and business seemed pale to Lewis in comparison to the pursuit of ideas. He claimed jokingly that if he were to go into business he would be bankrupt or in jail very soon. He didn't feel that following his father's footsteps into the law was the right decision either. Listening

In addition to the essence of ideas, Lewis valued his friendships. A few of his friends, sharing Lewis's interest in writing and philosophy, eventually formed a club with him that they called the Inklings. This small group met at a pub (their favourite was the Eagle and Child in Oxford, which they nicknamed the Bird and Baby) or at Lewis's rooms at the college to talk about

Lewis named Professor Digory Kirke (far left, as portrayed by Jim Broadbent in the movie The Lion, the Witch and the Wardrobe) after W. T. Kirkpatrick (oval photo at left), an old teacher of his father's who became Jack's private tutor and intellectual mentor at the age of fifteen.

World War I and its violent trench warfare (below) interrupted Jack's years at Oxford University. He enlisted in 1917 and was injured in France before he finally completed his education and became a lecturer at Oxford's Magdalen College (right).

[No. 10 British Red Cross Hospital,]
Le Tréport
22 February 1918

My dear Papy,

...I have discovered that optimism about the war increases in an inverse ratio to the optimist's proximity to the line...But indeed I'm afraid I must live up to our family reputation, for certainly I can't see any bright prospects at present...

your loving,
son Jack

In World War I, Lewis (on left, top photo) joined the Army's Officer Training Corps and met Paddy Moore (on the right). In the army (below, with comrades), Moore (prominent in foreground) and Lewis (partially hidden behind Moore) became best friends. When Moore was killed, Lewis cared for his friend's mother.

The war was brutal, and Lewis saw many of his friends killed.

literature. They often read aloud portions of whatever book each was writing to get feedback from their trusted peers. This distinguished group included Warnie, Owen Barfield, Charles Williams and J. R. R. Tolkien, who would one day write *The Lord of the Rings*.

In 1930, the Lewis brothers and Mrs Moore moved into a house in Oxford called The Kilns. It was a cosy home with beautiful surroundings that included a pond and extensive gardens. There also was room for Lewis's grandfather's wardrobe. Lewis wrote, "I have noticed since the very first night I slept here . . . that this house has a good night atmosphere about it: in the sense that I have never been in a place where one was *less* likely to get the creeps: a place less sinister. Good life

must have been lived here before us. If it is haunted, it is haunted by good spirits." Lewis told Greeves that he had never dared to hope for a house like it. He would live at The Kilns for the rest of his life.

Lewis was becoming quite famous as a scholar, lecturer, writer and speaker. As a teacher he was kind and patient but demanding and aggressive. He was always up for a good debate—and always set out to win. He gave speeches over the radio, and his deep voice was very recognizable. In his free time, Lewis loved getting together with his friends, travelling by train, visiting castles and monuments and taking walking tours. He also loved watching the deer in the park outside his office window at Magdalen College. And he loved books— not only what was on the pages but also

In World War II, the Blitz hit London, shrouding St Paul's Cathedral in smoke. Lewis opened his Oxford home to children fleeing the city.

the way books felt and looked. As Lewis got older, his idea of a perfect day became tea by the fire with a book.

World War II broke out in 1939, and the Germans soon began to pound London with nightly air raids. Lewis offered his house to a group of London children as a refuge from the bombing. He had always been uncomfortable around children, but when a few came to stay at The Kilns, Lewis was happy for their company. The presence of children at The Kilns seems to have inspired Lewis to start taking notes for what, in another nine years, would become *The Lion, the Witch and the Wardrobe*.

Lewis wrote, "This book is about four children whose names were Ann, Martin, Rose and Peter. But it is mostly about Peter who was the youngest. They all had to go away from London suddenly because of the Air Raids, and because Father, who was in the army, had gone off to the war and Mother was doing some kind of war work. They were sent to stay with a relation of Mother's who was a very old Professor who lived by himself in the country."

The war ended in 1945. Lewis had focused on writing for adults, putting aside his children's book for some years. But Lewis picked up his notes again in 1948 and renamed the children. Keeping the same

"Sacrifice almost everything to live where you can be near your friends."

With Paddy Moore gone and his own mother long dead, Lewis created a semblance of family life with Paddy's mother, Mrs Moore (on right in photo at left), and her daughter, Maureen.

In the movie The Lion, the Witch and the Wardrobe (opposite page, above), *a train is shown evacuating children to the country from wartime London. The Pevensie children are in the centre.*

Lewis infused *The Chronicles* with camaraderie and celebrated the strong ties among friends and siblings. He was grateful that he had the love of his brother, Warnie, and his close circle of friends.

In a letter to his best friend, Arthur Greeves, Lewis wrote, "[F]riendship is the greatest of worldly goods. Certainly to me it is the chief happiness of life. If I had to give a piece of advice to a young man about a place to live, I think I shd. [should] say, 'sacrifice almost everything to live where you can be near your friends.' I know I am v. [very] fortunate in that respect...."

concept as before, the book now began, "Once there were four children whose names were Peter, Susan, Edmund and Lucy. This story is about something that happened to them when they were sent away from London during the war because of the air-raids. They were sent to the house of an old Professor who lived in the heart of the country...."

Lewis read portions of the story to the Inklings for their opinion. Most were delighted by Lewis's tale, but Tolkien had a different perspective on how to create fantasy worlds. Tolkien felt the mythology of a world should be consistent and that Lewis was drawing from too many sources, mixing pagan creatures, such as Fauns and Centaurs, with Christian icons like Father Christmas. But it was impor-

tant to Lewis to fill Narnia with the things he loved, the things that represented for him the essence of life: talking animals, brave heroes, magical quests, high ethics, secret rooms, loyal friends, great adventures and the power of love.

Given the two driving forces in Lewis's life—the power of ideas and the power of friendship—it is not surprising that he

May 29th. 1954

Dear Fifth Graders

...I'm tall, fat, rather
bald, red-faced, double-
chinned, black-haired,
have a deep voice, and
wear glasses for reading...

Yours ever,
C.S. Lewis

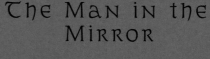

The Man in the Mirror

When Lewis was eight years old, he described himself in his diary. "I am like most boys of 8 and I am like Papy, bad temper, thick lips, thin, and generaly wearing a jersey....Hoora!" At the age of fifty-five, Lewis described himself in a letter for a class of American students (left).

and a close friend could argue passionately and very personally about the ideas within a book. Indeed, Tolkien and Lewis were to have many literary, philosophical and even personal arguments over the course of their lives, but they remained close friends in the end. In a move that seems to underscore the enduring affinity between Lewis and Tolkien, Lewis even chose Pauline Baynes to illustrate *The Chronicles of Narnia*. Baynes was the same young woman who had illustrated one of Tolkien's early books, *Father Giles of Ham*.

The years immediately following the decision to write *The Lion, the Witch and the Wardrobe* were marked by important events for Lewis. All seven books of *The Chronicles of Narnia* were written in this productive period. In 1951, Mrs Moore

died. She had been Lewis's friend and companion for more than three decades. In 1954, after thirty years at Oxford, Lewis became professor of medieval and Renaissance literature at Magdalene College of Cambridge, roughly eighty miles away. Lewis enjoyed this change in his life, saying the long train ride from The Kilns gave him time to read and think. Another more radical change occurred when he met an American woman named Joy Gresham. After a long friendship that eventually became a courtship, Joy Gresham married Lewis in a civil ceremony. He was fifty-seven.

Joy had two young sons from her previous marriage. David and Douglas had read Lewis's books and were excited to meet him. Douglas, as an adult writer, set down his memories of Lewis and his mother in the book *Lenten Lands*. He recalls being a little disappointed when, as a child, he first met the famous author. "Here was a man who was on speaking terms with King Peter, with the Great Lion, Aslan himself. Here was the man who had been to Narnia; surely he should at least wear silver chain mail and be girt about with a jewel-encrusted sword-belt."

After Joy tragically passed away from cancer just four years after her marriage to Lewis,

Lewis's health also began to deteriorate, and on November 22, 1963, on the same day that John F. Kennedy was assassinated, Jack Lewis died, having deeply affected the world by the way he lived his life and the words he left behind.

When he married Joy Gresham, Lewis was fifty-seven. In fair weather, the two loved to sit in the eight-acre garden of their home, The Kilns (below).

"Here was a man who was on speaking terms with King Peter . . ."

The Great Tale

—

C. S. Lewis devoted more than six years to writing the seven books of The Chronicles of Narnia, and it took him another four years before he determined the sequence in which the books should be read. He freely admitted that he hadn't planned to write a series. The story line of each successive book was as much a surprise to him as to his readers.

As it turned out, the books were written in one order, published in another and are meant to be read in yet another sequence. Over the years, this has given rise to considerable controversy because few people are familiar with Lewis's wishes.

Three Orders

There has been quite a bit of controversy over how the books in *The Chronicles of Narnia* should be read. Lewis had a preferred sequence (see list 3). Below is a complete set of first editions.

1. Lewis wrote the books in this order:
The Lion, the Witch and the Wardrobe, 1948
Prince Caspian, 1949
The Voyage of the Dawn Treader, 1950
The Horse and His Boy, 1950
The Silver Chair, 1951
The Last Battle, 1953
The Magician's Nephew, 1954

2. The books were published in this order:
The Lion, the Witch and the Wardrobe, 1950
Prince Caspian, 1951
The Voyage of the Dawn Treader, 1952
The Silver Chair, 1953
The Horse and His Boy, 1954
The Magician's Nephew, 1955
The Last Battle, 1956

3. Lewis wanted the books read in this order:
The Magician's Nephew
The Lion, the Witch and the Wardrobe
The Horse and His Boy
Prince Caspian
The Voyage of the Dawn Treader
The Silver Chair
The Last Battle

Lewis's decision about the correct sequence for reading *The Chronicles* was prompted by a young reader. Two years after *The Last Battle*, the final book in the series, was published in 1956, a boy named Laurence wrote to Lewis to suggest the books should be read chronologically according to Narnian time rather than in the order of their publication. Lewis supported this new sequence because it allowed the readers to keep better track of the "comings and goings between Narnia and our world".

Now all collections of *The Chronicles* are arranged in the order in which Laurence and Lewis agreed they should be read.

"[Y]ou must not believe all that authors tell you about how they wrote their books," Lewis once said. "This is not because they mean to tell lies. It is because a man writing a story is too excited about the story itself to sit back and notice how he is doing it."

As he wrote to Laurence, Lewis hadn't set out to write an entire series. Instead, the series grew on its own as Lewis discovered he had more to say. After writing *The Lion, the Witch and the Wardrobe*, Lewis immediately started taking notes on future books. One of them was intended to explain how the lamp-post wound up in Narnia and the origins of the White Witch. He called this one *Digory and Polly*, and would work on it on and off for the next few years to make sure it was exactly right. Meanwhile, Lewis turned his attention to other facets of Narnia.

He decided to explore the idea of people from our world being called into a *magical*

The adventure truly begins for the Pevensie children (opposite page, as seen in the movie The Lion, the Witch and the Wardrobe) *when they walk into the Witch's winter, wearing the coats they found in the wardrobe.*

Correspondence with Laurence, a young reader, led Lewis to revise the order in which the books of The Chronicles *should be read. The text of Lewis's response to Laurence (below left) clearly expresses the author's preference.*

April 23rd. [19]57

Dear Laurence

...I think I agree with your order for reading the books...The series was not planned beforehand...When I wrote The Lion, [the Witch and the Wardrobe], I did not know I was going to write any more. Then I wrote P. [rince] Caspian as a sequel and still didn't think there would be any more, and when I had done The Voyage [of the "Dawn Treader"] I felt quite sure it would be the last. But I found I was wrong...

yours
C. S. Lewis

world, rather than someone calling a magical creature out of its world into ours. Originally, he began this new book with the same first sentence as *The Lion, the Witch and the Wardrobe* ("Once there were four children…") and titled it *Drawn into Narnia*. It eventually became the only book with a subtitle, *Prince Caspian: The Return to Narnia*. This book, with its story-within-a-story format, is more complex than *The Lion, the Witch and the Wardrobe*, but the reader gets a much deeper understanding of Narnian history and of how the travellers from Earth affected it.

. . . the wild, briny smell . . . convinced Lucy that she was not dreaming.

The next book Lewis wrote, *The Voyage of the* Dawn Treader, came very easily as he loved writing about the sea. He had originally planned on having one of the Narnian characters come to Earth through the same picture that brought the children into Narnia but changed his mind. Fascinated by dreams, he revealed to his good friend Roger Lancelyn Green that the island where nightmares come true was based on his own lifelong battle with nightmares.

As Lewis's love of the sea inspired *The Voyage of the* Dawn Treader, his love of horses helped to create *The Horse and His Boy*. For this book, which is set in desert climates, he likely drew on his knowledge of the Arabian Nights, which according to one of his students, he had recently reread. This is the only book that doesn't include comings and goings between Earth and Narnia, and it takes place entirely within the world of Narnia and its neighbouring countries.

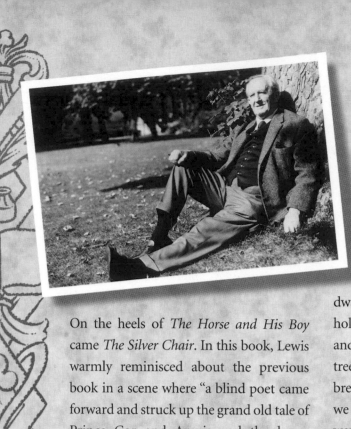

Lord of the Rings *author J. R. R. Tolkien* (left), *with Lewis, was a member of the Inklings, a small group who met regularly to share their interest in writing and philosophy.*

On the heels of *The Horse and His Boy* came *The Silver Chair.* In this book, Lewis warmly reminisced about the previous book in a scene where "a blind poet came forward and struck up the grand old tale of Prince Cor and Aravis and the horse Bree...." Lewis's publisher decided to publish *The Silver Chair* first, so instead of reminding readers of a book they had already read, this passage served to give his readers a glimpse of what was coming up in *The Chronicles.*

He then turned to what would be the final book in the series, *The Last Battle.* He told his publisher, "You will hear with mixed feelings that I have just finished the seventh and really the last of the Narnian stories."

But there was still the matter of finishing the book he had begun years before, the one that would tell the beginning of the Narnian tales. What had begun as *Digory and Polly* became *The Magician's Nephew.* Finally happy with the way the story turned out, Lewis handed in the full manuscript in 1954 and the series of seven books was done.

Lewis's friend J. R. R. Tolkien wrote that fantasy "contains many things besides elves and fays, and besides dwarfs, witches, trolls, giants, or dragons: it holds the seas, the sun, the moon, the sky; and the earth, and all things that are in it: tree and bird, water and stone, wine and bread, and ourselves, mortal men, when we are enchanted." Even though the books were not planned, they were executed so consistently that the romance, adventure and wonder of *The Chronicles of Narnia* build and intensify from the moment Aslan sings Narnia into existence in *The Magician's Nephew* to the moment he presides over its end in *The Last Battle.*

Lewis was a scholar and a deeply spiritual person, so it is no surprise that all his characters have to face the complex nature of the human condition. As a young boy, Lewis suffered terrible nightmares filled with ghosts and, as Lewis described them, "insects the size of small ponies". Lewis's terror of insects originated when he was only four or five years old. He was given a present of an elaborately made book that contained pop-up figures. When young Jack first opened the book, a huge paper spider sprang out at him. The nightmares began with that spider, according to the Lewis family.

Reading fantasy helped Lewis to deal with the fears that plagued him in real life. He believed fantasy makes it easier for all children to cope with their fears. In an essay in support of fantasy literature for children, he wrote, "Since it is so likely that they will meet cruel enemies [in real life], let them at least have heard of brave knights and heroic courage. Otherwise you are making their destiny not brighter but darker." By writing about serious themes like distrust, pride, temptation and greed in a fantastical environment, Lewis helps readers to recognize these emotions and forces in their own lives. In each book, pivotal events arise when characters face such forces and are required to either take command of their own lives or surrender. The fateful decisions they make determine the direction and outcome of the story.

What's in a Name?

Before deciding on the titles of each book in *The Chronicles*, Lewis generally considered a raft of ideas. Here are a few of the alternative titles that never made it onto a book cover. It is easy to see which books were hardest to name.

Some alternative titles considered by C. S. Lewis and his publisher	The final title of the book
Digory and Polly	*The Magician's Nephew*
Narnia and the North, The Desert Road to Narnia, The Horse and the Boy, Cor of Archenland, The Horse Stole the Boy, Over the Border, The Horse Bree…and more	*The Horse and His Boy*
Drawn into Narnia, A Horn in Narnia	*Prince Caspian*
Night under Narnia, Wild Waste Lands	*The Silver Chair*
The Last King of Narnia, Night Falls on Narnia, The Last Chronicle of Narnia	*The Last Battle*

The Magician's Nephew

As Lewis's letter to Laurence reveals, a single sweeping saga is presented in the seven books of *The Chronicles*—a saga that can be viewed as one long tale. This great tale begins in the year 1900 in *The Magician's Nephew*, when two young friends and neighbours, Digory and Polly, fall prey to a scheme of Digory's wicked uncle Andrew. Using enchanted dust from the lost land of Atlantis, Andrew has fashioned magic rings that can transport people to worlds beyond our universe. But Andrew is afraid to use the rings himself. Needing suitable test subjects, Andrew seizes on the two children.

The rings magically transport Digory and Polly to a place they call the Wood between the Worlds, where each of many ponds leads to another world. They choose one and it takes them to Charn, a world that has been destroyed by the evil Witch Jadis.

Jadis returns to London with Polly and Digory and creates chaos. The children try to get her away from Earth. They take their chances and magically depart for an unknown destination, taking a cab horse, the cabman and Uncle Andrew with them. They all are pulled into a world that doesn't yet exist—a place of total darkness. But then Aslan, the Great Lion, appears and sings Narnia and everything in it into being in a glorious display of colour and sound. As Polly says, it seemed everything was coming "out of the Lion's head". Listening to the Lion sing and watching the land, Polly and Digory and the others see the plants and the animals come into existence.

Digory is given a chance to save his dying mother, but only if he can prove himself worthy through a series of heroic acts. He passes the test, and he and Polly are transported back to Earth carrying a magic apple from a Narnian tree. The apple cures Digory's mother, and the boy plants the apple's core. It grows into a wondrous apple tree just as Digory is growing up to become Professor Kirke, who eventually builds a very unusual wardrobe from the wood of that otherworldly tree.

Digory Contends with Evil

The human struggle against the temptation

A Sense of Longing

When Lewis was a very young boy, he first recognized a feeling that would play an integral role in his thoughts and writings throughout his life. From his first bedroom window in Belfast he stared out at the green line of the Castlereagh Hills—beautiful pastures that he was too young to explore—and he felt immersed in his longing to go there. This sense of longing runs through all Lewis's writing and forms the emotional core of *The Chronicles*.

Lewis's longing was focused on the beauty and seemingly unattainable perfection of nature. But instead of allowing this feeling to overwhelm him with emptiness, he felt it as great joy—the unadulterated joy of sharing the world with such natural wonders. An early crafts project introduced him to this new emotion. His brother, Warnie, had built a garden inside the lid of a biscuit tin that he covered in moss, flowers and twigs.

...a sea of tossing gold...

Lewis wistfully wrote, "As long as I live my imagination of Paradise will retain something of my brother's toy garden." Lewis credits this garden with bringing him his first experience of a type of joy that he didn't know existed—that which stems from something tangible, like nature, and then takes up residence in the imagination.

He wanted to pass this feeling along to his readers. With the character of Aslan, Lewis breathed life into the concept of longing. Describing Digory and Polly's experience of the Great Lion, Lewis wrote: "[Aslan's] face seemed to be a sea of tossing gold in which they were floating, and such a sweetness and power rolled about them and over them and entered them that they felt they had never really been happy or wise or good, or even alive and awake, before. And the memory of that moment stayed with them always, so that as long as they both lived, if ever they were sad or afraid or angry, the thought of all that golden goodness, and the feeling that it was still there, quite close, just round some corner or just behind some door, would come back and make them sure, deep down inside, that all was well."

Lewis wrote, "When I was ten, I read fairy tales in secret and would have been ashamed if I had been found doing so. Now that I am fifty I read them openly." Lewis felt that this yearning for fairy land is a special kind of longing. "Does anyone suppose that he really and prosaically longs for all the dangers and discomforts of a fairy tale?—really wants dragons in contemporary England? It is not so. It would be much truer to say that fairy land arouses a longing for he knows not what….[T]he boy reading the fairy tale desires and is happy in the very fact of desiring. For his mind has not been concentrated on himself, as it often is in the more realistic story."

The great tale of Narnia first unfolded behind the covers of these first editions of The Chronicles' seven books, all illustrated by Pauline Baynes.

As bombs fall on London (opposite), Susan hugs Lucy while their mother comforts her youngest son, Edmund, in a scene from the movie The Lion, the Witch and the Wardrobe.

to do evil was a theme that Lewis wrote and spoke about many times. Writing to a friend in spring 1942, as World War II raged, Lewis paraphrased the nineteenth-century theologian Bishop Brooke Foss Westcott, saying, "Only he who completely resists temptation knows its true strength." Lewis explained, "If you give in at point X you never know how fierce it [would] have become an hour later. You only discover the strength of the German army by fighting it." The difficulty of resisting temptation is a central theme of *The Magician's Nephew*. Twice—at the very beginning and

the conclusion—Digory is faced with temptation, and the course of history hangs on his ability to resist.

As the book opens in the ruined city of Charn, Digory is both tempted and warned by magical words carved on a stone pillar:

Make your choice, adventurous Stranger;
Strike the bell and bide the danger,
Or wonder, till it drives you mad,
What would have followed if you had.

Although he knows better and Polly begs him not to, Digory gives in to the temptation and strikes the bell. His act frees Jadis from the spell that bound her, and this allows her to spread her evil into Narnia.

The terrible consequences of his surrender to temptation plague Digory throughout the book, as he first sees Narnia created in pure goodness and then must deal with the Witch's introduction of evil into the new world. When he is warned not to taste the magic apple that might cure his mother, Digory uses reason, not his emotions, to think through what he must do to resist and succeed.

THE LION, THE WITCH AND THE WARDROBE

As *The Lion, the Witch and the Wardrobe* opens, a thousand years have passed in Narnia but only forty years have gone by on Earth. England and all Europe are in the grip of World War II. Four siblings—Peter, Susan, Edmund and Lucy Pevensie —are sent to the country to stay with old professor Digory Kirke to escape the air raids in London.

The children step through the professor's wardrobe and find themselves in the land of Narnia, which has fallen under the evil rule of the White Witch. Because of the Witch, it is always winter but never Christmas in Narnia. Enchanted by the Witch's offer of endless Turkish Delight and a chance to be King, Edmund betrays his brother, sisters and the Great Lion, Aslan.

For the first time in many years, Aslan appears in Narnia and reveals himself to possess the knowledge of all three levels of magic: Magic, the Deep Magic and, most powerful of all, the Deeper Magic, a set of eternal, universal principles known only to

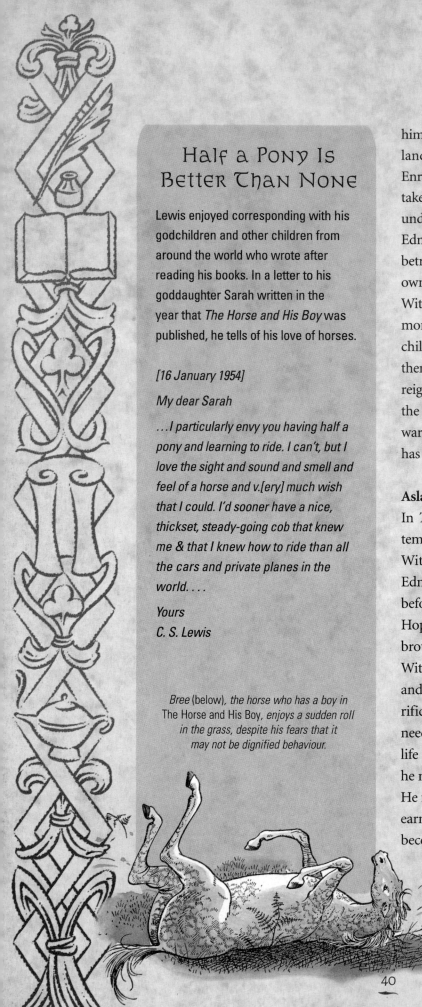

Half a Pony Is Better Than None

Lewis enjoyed corresponding with his godchildren and other children from around the world who wrote after reading his books. In a letter to his goddaughter Sarah written in the year that *The Horse and His Boy* was published, he tells of his love of horses.

[16 January 1954]

My dear Sarah

…I particularly envy you having half a pony and learning to ride. I can't, but I love the sight and sound and smell and feel of a horse and v.[ery] much wish that I could. I'd sooner have a nice, thickset, steady-going cob that knew me & that I knew how to ride than all the cars and private planes in the world. . . .

Yours
C. S. Lewis

Bree (below), *the horse who has a boy in* The Horse and His Boy, *enjoys a sudden roll in the grass, despite his fears that it may not be dignified behaviour.*

him. Aslan brings summer back to the land, vanquishing the Witch's winter. Enraged, the Witch demands her right to take Edmund's life—a right she is owed under the rules of the Deep Magic because Edmund has yielded to temptation and betrayed his siblings. But Aslan offers his own life in place of Edmund's. After the Witch kills him, Aslan returns to life even more powerful than before. He helps the children defeat the Witch and crowns them Kings and Queens of Narnia. After reigning over the Golden Age of Narnia, the children return home through the wardrobe—only to find that no time at all has passed on Earth.

Aslan's Sacrifice Saves Edmund's Soul

In *The Lion, the Witch and the Wardrobe*, temptation takes the form of the White Witch's enchanted Turkish Delight. Edmund barely struggles with his greed before giving in and accepting the sweet. Hoping for more, he agrees to betray his brother and sisters in order to stay in the Witch's favour. His greed puts his siblings and all Narnia in great danger. Aslan's sacrifice gives Edmund the second chance he needs for redemption. Granted continued life by Aslan, Edmund acknowledges that he made bad choices and is very ashamed. He fights bravely against the Witch's army, earns back the trust of his siblings and becomes a King of Narnia at their sides.

The Horse and His Boy

In the land of Calormen, far to the south of Narnia, a young boy named Shasta realizes that the man who raised him is not his real father. In Narnia, it is the Golden Age and the four Pevensie children reign justly and well in Cair Paravel. But in Calormen, the evil Tisroc rules despotically. Shasta runs away from his false father, riding a talking horse named Bree who was kidnapped from Narnia many years earlier. Shasta and Bree are joined by Aravis, a privileged Calormene girl fleeing an arranged marriage, and her friend, the talking horse Hwin, who also is Narnian. Together, the four escape north to Narnia.

The journey is filled with danger as the small group makes its way over tall mountains and the expansive desert. With Aslan's help, they arrive in Archenland, the

The evil White Witch cursed Narnia with eternal winter, portrayed here in a photo from the movie The Lion, the Witch and the Wardrobe. *But Aslan brought spring and the rule of goodness back to Narnia.*

country directly south of Narnia, in time to warn the people of an attack that would have destroyed both Archenland and Narnia. Shasta learns that good King Lune of Archenland is his real father and that he is a prince, the twin brother of his new friend Prince Corin.

Truth Overcomes Prejudice

Both the children and the horses have to put aside their prejudices and trust one another in order to survive the dangers of their journey and save Narnia.

Bree, who has proclaimed that he hates lions and doesn't believe that Aslan could be such a beast, is called to set aside his deepest prejudices. Bree's conversion takes place near the book's end when Aslan shows himself to the talking stallion. Faced with the truth of Aslan's existence, Bree tells the Lion who saved Narnia, "I'm afraid I must be rather a fool." Aslan responds, "Happy the Horse who knows that while he is still young. Or the Human either."

The only character who refuses to base his judgments on knowledge is Rabadash, the evil Calormene prince who is set on conquering Narnia and Archenland. Aslan gives Rabadash a chance to put his hatred to rest, but he refuses. Aslan turns Rabadash into a donkey, explaining that the prince will be returned to and remain in his human form only so long as he stays within ten miles of the great temple of Tash in Tashbaan. Aslan confines the prince to a small portion of Calormen.

PRINCE CASPIAN

In *Prince Caspian* another thirteen hundred years have passed in Narnia since the Golden Age when Peter, Susan, Edmund and Lucy reigned. However, just one year has gone by on Earth. In Narnia, the Telmarines have overrun the land and pushed the Talking Beasts of Old Narnia into near extinction. Most humans no longer believe the magical, talking creatures of Narnia ever existed or that Aslan is real. The Narnian realm has been diverted from the goodness of its old ways by a wicked new order. As civil war threatens the land, the four children are called back to Narnia to help Prince Caspian, the rightful heir to the Narnian throne, overthrow his evil uncle Miraz, restore peace to the land and return Narnia to the path of goodness and truth.

A Return to the Old Narnian Virtues

Under its new, arrogant rulers, Narnia has gone astray. In *Prince Caspian*, Lewis explores the land's struggle to restore its original values, particularly the virtue of humility and the grace that underlies it. Through the actions of two very different characters, Lewis shows that those who would perform great deeds need the humility to feel unworthy of the heroic roles cast for them.

Dwarf's deep battle wound. Trumpkin then gracefully acknowledges he was wrong to doubt them. "My humble duty to your Majesties all—humble duty," he says. He is quickly and happily forgiven.

A greater lesson in humility is delivered at the climax of the story, when Aslan, preparing to crown Caspian

The poor dragon that had been Eustace lifted up its voice and wept.

In The Voyage of the Dawn Treader, *Eustace is magically turned into a dragon by his own greedy thoughts. Suddenly missing friends and companionship for the first time, Eustace the dragon* (above) *weeps.*

Although he believes the mission to be a "wild goose chase", the Dwarf Trumpkin, a loyal adviser to the prince, volunteers to travel to the ruins of Cair Paravel to await the possible return of the Royal Children from Earth. Trumpkin is too proud and stubborn to believe that four children can offer any real help to his embattled land. But a series of events demonstrates the children's power: Edmund defeats the dwarfish warrior in a duel, Susan proves herself a great archer and Lucy magically cures the

as Narnia's new King, asks him if he feels ready to accept the throne. Even though Prince Caspian has just helped to unite a warring Narnia, he says no. "I—I don't think I do, Sir. I'm only a kid."

Pleased, Aslan responds, "Good. If you had felt yourself sufficient, it would have been a proof that you were not."

The humble Caspian is then crowned King of Narnia.

THE VOYAGE OF THE DAWN TREADER

As *The Voyage of the* Dawn Treader begins, just three more years have passed in Narnia

With Respect to Those Who Came Before

In the Narnia books, Lewis paid homage to fantasy writer E. (Edith) Nesbit, one of his boyhood favourites. Nesbit wrote many books for children in the late nineteenth and early twentieth centuries, including a trilogy of adventures about the Bastable siblings that began with *The Story of the Treasure Seekers*, and fantasies such as *The Five Children and It*. In 1948, Lewis told a friend that he was working on a children's book "in the tradition of E. Nesbit". Nearly ten years later, he wrote in a letter to a young fan, "I love E. Nesbit too and I think I have learned a lot from her about how to write stories of this kind."

In her book *The Story of the Amulet*, Nesbit put her own name in the story as a joke: "What was the name the Queen said? Nisbeth—Nesbit—something?" Lewis wrote in the beginning of *The Magician's Nephew*, "In those days…the Bastables were looking for treasure in the Lewisham Road"—thereby getting in two subtle nods to Nesbit in one fell swoop.

Fellow fantasy author George MacDonald was another of Lewis's favourite writers. Lewis praised MacDonald often: "I have never concealed the fact that I regarded him as my master; indeed I fancy I have never written a book in which I did not quote from him."

MacDonald demonstrates that a fantasy story for children can have many layers of significance, even if the reader doesn't realize it at the time. For instance, his tale *At the Back of the North Wind* is the story of how the North Wind visits a small boy and takes him travelling. But it also is the story of the circle of life and death. Similarly, *The Chronicles of Narnia* function as a multilevel metaphor for the great mysteries of existence, and the careful reader will continue to see more of that metaphor revealed with each reading.

and one in England. Edmund, Lucy and their obnoxious cousin Eustace are magically pulled through a painting of a sailing ship and are taken aboard the *Dawn Treader*, King Caspian's ship. Caspian is searching for his murdered father's seven loyal friends, great lords who disappeared after being sent on a dangerous mission by the evil King Miraz (who was killed in the final pages of *Prince Caspian*). As they search the unexplored Eastern islands for the missing men, Caspian and the children have many great and strange adventures, and eventually approach the World's End and the border of Aslan's country.

The Search for Something Bigger

Everyone in *The Voyage of the* Dawn Treader is on a search—for lost lords, cherished friendship or some other goal. The

44

Mr Tumnus thinks Lucy is from the country "Spare Oom".

Lucy Pevensie and Mr Tumnus the Faun greet each other in the movie The Lion, the Witch and the Wardrobe.

most dramatic search, especially as the book reaches its climax, is Reepicheep's quest for Aslan's country—a deeply spiritual search for a land that no one has ever seen.

As the voyagers explore the Eastern Sea, love and its power to work great change also are explored. One of the greatest transformations in *The Chronicles* is that of Eustace Clarence Scrubb, who, as Lewis writes at the start of the book, "almost deserved" to have that awful name. Eustace is a petulant, spoiled boy who cares only for himself. When he finds a dragon's treasure, he plots ways to steal it. His greed actually turns him into a dragon, and he becomes lonely and depressed. As a dragon, he realizes the comfort of friendship and how good it feels to help others. Once he has proved himself worthy, Aslan tears away the dragon skin and Eustace is reborn—both literally and figuratively.

Eustace lives out the book's central idea by finding himself and then going on to become a very different, greatly improved person. Caspian locates three of the lords he was seeking and, at the same time, a wife, who joins him in establishing a long-lived dynasty. We do not discover in *The Voyage of the* Dawn Treader exactly what it is that Reepicheep finds beyond the curve of the great green wave at the World's End. But we believe that he, too, has found what he was seeking and been transformed by it.

THE SILVER CHAIR

The Silver Chair begins fifty Narnian years after the *Dawn Treader*'s voyage of discovery, though only a few months have passed in England. The much-transformed Eustace and his friend Jill Pole escape their horrible boarding school by walking through a mysteriously unlocked door in a stone wall that leads to Narnia. Aslan assigns the

"I'm on Aslan's side

It is the faith of Puddleglum the Marsh-wiggle that saves the day in The Silver Chair.

she captures them, too. The book climaxes when the children and Puddleglum are enchanted by Underland's queen into believing that Narnia and Aslan are only a dream and lose all hope. But with Puddleglum leading the way, they are able to break the terrible spell.

A Marsh-wiggle Proves the Power of Faith

As the battle to overcome evil in Narnia continues, *The Silver Chair* is a tale about the paramount importance of trust and faith, without which the children and Rilian would have been lost forever in the pit of Underland. It is a lack of trust in both Aslan and themselves that causes Jill and Eustace to miss Aslan's signs. They don't understand the signs and have little faith that they will recognize them. So they don't. As the story progresses, their trust in each other grows and, with it, their ability to recognize Aslan's signs and to see reality clearly.

children a mission: Find Caspian's missing son, Rilian. They are given four signs to guide them, but manage to miss most of these signals. Still, with the always gloomy but valiant Marsh-wiggle Puddleglum as their guide, they track Rilian to the underground kingdom of Underland. There they must rescue him from the evil Witch-queen, the Lady of the Green Kirtle, before

In the end, it is Puddleglum's faith in goodness that breaks the Witch's evil, enchanted hold on him and his companions. The Witch has cast a spell on Puddleglum, Jill, Eustace and Rilian, making the four believe that Narnia and Aslan don't really exist and that the sun and the stars are delusions.

even if there isn't any Aslan to lead it."

But Puddleglum manages to shake off the spell long enough to bravely stamp out the fire with his bare, webbed foot, inflicting considerable pain on himself. His sacrifice works. With the fire nearly out, the enchanted smoke dissipates and the pain itself clears the Marsh-wiggle's head. Suddenly "he knew exactly what he really thought". In this clearheaded instant, Puddleglum concludes that what the Witch is saying doesn't matter because both the Lion and the land stand for goodness—and Puddleglum has faith in the power and the rightness of good.

"Suppose we *have* only dreamed, or made up, all those things—trees and grass and sun and moon and stars and Aslan himself….Then all I can say is that, in that case, the made-up things seem a good deal more important than the real ones….I'm on Aslan's side even if there isn't any Aslan to lead it," Puddleglum tells Underland's Queen. And the spell is broken by the Marsh-wiggle's faith and courage.

THE LAST BATTLE

In *The Last Battle*, the final book of the series, two hundred years have passed in Narnia

and seven on Earth when the evil ape Shift forces the gentle donkey Puzzle to impersonate Aslan in order to take over Narnia. Good King Tirian calls for help, and Eustace and Jill are called into Narnia. Together they fight a great battle to save Narnia—but it is a battle they can't win. Aslan arrives with all the good friends of Narnia. He allows darkness to fall on Narnia forever, and he leads all the loyal people and creatures into a new world— the real Narnia of Aslan's country.

Lewis described the new Narnia of Aslan's country metaphorically as a lovely landscape glimpsed briefly in a mirror that makes everything look "deeper, more wonderful, more like places in a story: in a story you have never heard but very much want to know". But Lewis leaves it to the Unicorn to describe the new Narnia directly: "I have come home at last! This is my real country! I belong here. This is the land I have been looking for all my life, though I never knew it till now."

Then Aslan spoke to all the creatures and people. "And as He spoke He no longer looked to them like a lion; but the things that began to happen after that were so great and beautiful that I cannot write them," Lewis wrote.

One World Ends, the Future Begins
As the great tale of Narnia comes to a

close, Lewis seems to emphasize once more that faith and trust have the power to create the future, while the lack of them can destroy it.

Shift asserts that in the absence of Aslan, his superior nature means that *he* should be the ruler of the land, and he insists that the Calormene god Tash is behind him. Shift convinces so many people and beasts that even the King and the friends of Narnia can't overcome the evil that has crept into the land. In the end, however, Shift's struggle for power dooms him, along with all the others who turned their back on the goodness of Narnia. As Narnia is dying, Aslan offers them a new home, but most don't accept it, either out of fear, obstinacy or hatred.

One soldier named Emeth chooses a different path than the rest. A faithful servant of Tash, whom he believed to be the source of goodness, Emeth chooses to follow Aslan out of the dying Narnia and into the unknown. It is an act of profound trust in the truth of goodness—and, indeed, "emeth" is the Hebrew word for "firmness", "faithfulness" and "truth".

The
Magic Lands
of Narnia

~

Open the pages of any book in The Chronicles and Narnia springs to life, stretching to the magical horizons of its alien lands and seas.

In C. S. Lewis's vivid descriptions, readers hear the snow crunch underfoot in the Lantern Waste, smell the sea air off the bow of the Dawn Treader, feel the chill breeze that blows off the towering, cloud-shrouded cliffs and suffer in the dank heat that rises from the rivers of fire in the underground realm. The landscapes and seascapes of the Narnian world seem as alive and real as any of the characters.

...these places are as critical to "The Chronicles" as any character...

Lewis wanted to create a world that did not feel fictional. He wanted readers to believe that Narnia might truly exist on the other side of a coat-filled wardrobe or just past the frame of a painting where an exotic ship sails. To create this fantastical, convincing world, Lewis combined real places with his imagination. He produced a landscape that was familiar and yet completely unlike any place on Earth.

For centuries, many people wrongly believed Earth to be flat. In Narnia, the same belief prevails, but we have no way of knowing the truth. Reepicheep says in *The Voyage of the* Dawn Treader that Narnia is "like a great round table and the waters of all the oceans endlessly pouring over the edge". When Reepicheep actually does sail to the World's End in *The Voyage of the Dawn Treader*, he finds a steep, green wave, like a wall of water. Still, the Narnian adventurer, like his historic earthly counterparts, expresses his belief that anyone who sails too far in any direction may fall over the edge of the planet.

To help guide travellers through Narnia, Lewis collaborated with the illustrator Pauline Baynes to develop detailed maps matching the events in each book. The maps help the reader visualize the land and follow the geography of the stories in ways that anchor the world of Narnia in seeming reality. Over the years, these maps have become an intrinsic part of the stories. Tracing them helps the reader travel the routes that connect the magical places in Lewis's world—from the old city of London, where the great tale begins, to the apparently tiny, dilapidated stable where *The Last Battle*, and the old Narnia, come to an end.

Here, then, are the most memorable of the places in *The Chronicles*, beginning in England right here on Earth, and ranging into Narnia and the neighbouring lands of that world.

This Side of the Wardrobe

The Chronicles of Narnia actually begin in our *own* world, in **London**, at the turn of the twentieth century. In 1900, people still used horses and carriages to travel the bustling cobblestoned streets. It is here that *The Magician's Nephew* begins. A cold, wet summer gives neighbours Digory and Polly the perfect excuse to stay inside and explore the connected attics of the terraced houses where they live. They realize they can get from one house to the next without going outdoors and set out to discover what secrets are hidden in the empty house next to Digory's. But they never make it past Digory's own attic, where an even bigger adventure awaits them.

In 1900, Lewis himself was a very young boy growing up in Belfast. It rained often, which gave him lots of time for what he called "indoor exploration". Lewis chose to set the first book of *The Chronicles* around the time of his own boyhood because he believed it was a more innocent period than the years surrounding the Second World War, when the other stories of *The Chronicles* take place. As the next book begins some forty years later, the war is raging and London has become too dangerous for children—even for children destined to be Kings and Queens of Narnia.

Professor Kirke's house is the country home where the Pevensie children are sent

When The Chronicles *began, the best way around London was by horse-drawn cabs, many of which were festooned with advertisements* (below).

The Professor's large country house (above)— pictured in a drawing for the movie of The Lion, the Witch and the Wardrobe—holds the magic wardrobe that first takes the Pevensie children to Narnia. Lewis based the Professor's house in part on Little Lea (inset left), his own boyhood home in Belfast.

The lamp-post in the Lantern Waste (opposite page, from the Disney-Walden Media film) may have been inspired by a country park near Lewis's boyhood home.

at the beginning of *The Lion, the Witch and the Wardrobe*. It belongs to Professor Digory Kirke (yes, *that* Digory), and an otherwise empty room upstairs is the site of the magic wardrobe. The Professor's house was inspired by Lewis's boyhood home, Little Lea, which also had long halls, spare rooms and passageways.

Experiment House is the school that Eustace and Jill unhappily attend on Earth. There isn't much learning or many rules, and the bullies get away with picking on everyone else. The school echoes some of Lewis's experiences as a young student, and it serves as an example of his belief that some teachers, in trying to be modern, neglect such diverse essentials of a classical education as discipline, maths, grammar and proper manners.

The Other Side

The first otherworldly place that the heroes of *The Chronicles* visit is the **Wood between the Worlds**, an enchanted wood where Digory and Polly find themselves after being tricked by Digory's uncle. As Lewis describes it in *The Magician's Nephew*, the wood is totally quiet—"You could almost feel the trees growing". Every few yards there is a pool of water, each leading to a different world. Digory describes it as "a *rich* place: as rich as plum-cake". The trees grow so thickly it is impossible to see the sky, but a strong sun filters through the leafy covering, suffusing the wood with warm, green light. Something about the place muddles the memory, because, at first, Digory and Polly don't recognize each other and recall nothing of their lives. They believe they have been in the wood forever. Luckily, their memories are jogged by seeing the subject of one of Uncle Andrew's prior experiments in magical travel—a guinea pig wearing one of the magic rings, which is tied to the small animal with a ribbon. Instantly the children remember everything.

Digory and Polly leap into one of the pools in the Wood between the Worlds and are transported to **Charn**, once a highly populated land known as the "city of the King of Kings", and the "wonder of the world, perhaps all worlds". But, by the time they arrive, the stone walls are crumbling and the courtyards are empty. Tall doorways lead to huge, cold rooms. The rivers have turned to dust, the sun is a dull red and the inhabitants are all dead, except for the Queen, who is frozen

in an enchanted sleep. When, much later, Aslan takes Digory and Polly back to the Wood between the Worlds, the pool to the ruined city has disappeared and the Lion warns the children that evil destroyed Charn and may also destroy Earth one day. "'When you were last here,' said Aslan, 'that hollow was a pool, and when you jumped into it you came to the world where a dying sun shone over the ruins of Charn. There is no pool now. That world is ended, as if it had never been. Let the race of Adam and Eve take warning.'"

The Creation of Narnia

When Digory and Polly first enter Narnia from London—along with the Cabby; his horse, Strawberry; Digory's wicked uncle Andrew; and the evil Witch Jadis—there is nothing to see. Besides the hard ground underneath them, there is only silence and blackness. Then they hear a song that has no words and seems to be coming from all around them. It is the most beautiful sound the children have ever heard. "The Cabby and the two children had open mouths and shining eyes; they were drinking in the sound, and they looked as if it reminded them of something," Lewis wrote.

The song seems to create the stars and the sun. The visitors can see that the singer of the amazing song is a huge, shaggy Lion who later introduces himself as Aslan. As the Lion walks and sings, the land comes alive with trees and flowers and grass that runs "up the sides of the little hills like a wave". As the song changes, humps appear in the ground and animals of all sizes and shapes burst out. Magical creatures such as Fauns and Dwarfs and Satyrs step out from the trees. Aslan stops and calls out, "Narnia, Narnia, Narnia, awake. Love. Think. Speak. Be walking trees. Be talking beasts. Be divine waters."

Even though evil has already entered Narnia in the form of the Witch Jadis, Aslan decrees, "For many hundred years yet this shall be a merry land in a merry world." And so it was, just as Aslan said, for many, many years.

Edmund Pevensie (right), *in a battle scene from the movie* The Lion, the Witch and the Wardrobe, *first enters Narnia through Lantern Waste.*

"Let the race of Adam and Eve take warning."

Lantern Waste marks the westernmost boundary of Narnia. These woods are home to Talking Trees, Dryads and Nymphs and the White Witch. Tumnus the Faun's cave home is here, as is Stable Hill. The Great Waterfall with its always-bubbling Caldron Pool lies on the western edge and feeds the Great River, which runs through the Lantern Waste all the way to the sea. Lantern Waste is the first place the Pevensie siblings see when they come through the wardrobe and the last place they see before Aslan ushers them into the Real Narnia at the end of *The Last Battle*. The lamp-post in the middle of the woods serves as an important landmark to the Narnians and the children alike.

Where did Lewis get the idea of putting a lamp-post in the middle of the woods? Some ten miles northeast of Belfast in the village of Crawfordsburn near the Irish Sea is Crawfordsburn Country Park. The park is not far from Lewis's boyhood home,

Little Lea, and he frequented the place for much of his life. There, in the middle of the wood, stands a lamp-post which may have been one of the inspirations for the most famous landmark in Lantern Waste. Such isolated lamp-posts are not as uncommon as one might think. In Cambridge, an old Victorian lamp-post stands alone in the middle of a field surrounded by trees. But while it, too, resembles the Narnian lamp-post, Lewis did not become very familiar with Cambridge until after he wrote *The Chronicles*.

Cair Paravel, the castle from which the High Kings and Queens rule Narnia, sits high on a hill, on a peninsula near where the mouth of the Great River meets the Great Eastern Ocean. The castle's Great Hall houses the fabled four thrones where the Pevensies are crowned. The hall's western wall is draped with tapestries and peacock feathers; from its eastern wall, a doorway looks out across the sea. Beneath the castle is the treasure

"The most ancient and most deeply magical" place in Narnia is the Stone Table (above, in a concept drawing for the movie The Lion, the Witch and the Wardrobe), *where Aslan is killed by the White Witch and then comes to life again.*

In creating the Stone Table, Lewis was influenced by the many standing stones—dolmens—erected throughout Ireland by prehistoric peoples. The dolmens, like this one (opposite page), *mark grave sites and served other ceremonial purposes.*

Narnia on Earth

Many of the locations in Narnia are based on real places that Lewis visited, read about or dreamed of in his youth. When he was a boy at Little Lea, he and Warnie used to ride their bikes through the Holywood Hills in County Down. At the crest, they could see the Mourne Mountains. Warnie believed this view inspired his brother to design the landscape of Narnia. Lewis himself pointed to the Carlingford Mountains above Carlingford Lough, an inlet on the east coast of Ireland. Lewis reported that these deepwater inlets and ancient hills, covered with wildflowers in the summer, most resemble the landscape of Narnia in his mind. He was also inspired by the bucolic surroundings of his own home in Oxford, The Kilns.

Scattered throughout Ireland are the stone traces of Celtic civilization, some dating back more than 4,000 years. Among the many ancient structures are the dolmens, two or more standing stones with a capstone balanced atop as a roof—thought to be grave sites. They fascinated Lewis and may have provided some inspiration for the Stone Table upon which Aslan is sacrificed in *The Lion, the Witch and the Wardrobe*.

As a child, Lewis loved the old castles that dot the Irish landscape. Ireland has scores of castles, most dating back hundreds of years. None are more famous than Carrickfergus Castle near Belfast, built in the twelfth century and reputed to be the first real Irish castle. Farther north near Portrush, Dunluce Castle, high on a rugged cliff, looks over the open sea.

As an adult, Lewis travelled throughout the British Isles to visit castles and ancient sites. Lewis and his friend Roger Lancelyn Green made a trip to the north of Wales to see the walled town of Conwy and Conwy Castle. The town dates from the late 1200s and the castle from the fourteenth century. Conwy is very similar to another castle in Wales, Beaumaris, on the island of Anglesey, barely a forty-minute drive from Conwy. Any and all of these seaside castles could have been models for Cair Paravel.

room where the children keep the special gifts they were given when they first arrived in Narnia. Suits of armour stand guard over the treasure room, which also houses precious jewels and golden objects.

When the children return to Narnia in *Prince Caspian*, it is hundreds of years after their reign. The castle is in ruins and almost completely unrecognizable. Apple trees have encroached on the castle's north wall and the land, formerly a peninsula, has

The castle of Cair Paravel on its little hill towered up above them....

Lewis's creation of Cair Paravel was based in part on the many castles of Ireland, Wales and England that he visited as a youth and an adult. Beaumaris Castle on Anglesey Island, Wales, is a thirteenth-century castle that Lewis visited.

WILDLANDS of the NORT

Miraz his Castle

Beaversdam

NARNIA

Cair Paravel

SSWATER

Narnia's Neighbours

In *The Chronicles*, Lewis describes the countries surrounding Narnia, along with the islands in the Great Eastern Ocean. Each place has its own geography, people and history, just as Narnia does.

Although it is never shown on any of the maps that Lewis and Baynes drew, Telmar is located on the other side of the mountain range that runs along Narnia's western border. It is west of the Lantern Waste, behind the great falls. According to the time line of events that Lewis constructed, in the Narnian year 460 a group of pirates from Earth wandered into a cave that was one of the chinks between Earth and Narnia. The pirates emerged from the cave in Telmar and settled the uninhabited land. About 1500 years later, their descendants, the Telmarines, conquered Narnia. They controlled it for 300 years before being defeated by Caspian's army in *Prince Caspian*.

Directly to the south of Narnia is a very small country called Archenland. In *The Horse and His Boy*, Archenland is ruled by good King Lune, who is a descendant of Narnia's earliest inhabitants—the London cabby, Frank, and his wife, Helen, crowned the first King and Queen of the land by Aslan. Rolling hills, snow-covered mountains, and many kinds of trees dot the Archenland landscape. The Castle at Anvard is King Lune's seat of power. Archenland and Narnia are allies.

Archenland is separated from its southern neighbour, Calormen, by a huge desert. The country was founded by Archenland bandits who escaped across the sands.

The Wild Lands of the North are directly north of Narnia, separated by the River Shribble. Closest to Narnia is Ettinsmoor, and north of this desolate, lonely area is Harfang, the name of a mountain and a castle that is home to bad giants who try to eat Eustace, Jill and Puddleglum in *The Silver Chair*.

Lewis, who loved Jules Verne's *Journey to the Centre of the Earth* and H. Rider Haggard's *King Solomon's Mines*, was undoubtedly influenced by these classics when he created his own underground world below Harfang, called Underland. Underland is composed of three distinct realms, the shallowest of which is called the Marches. All but the deepest parts are also known as the Shallow Lands, so named by those who dwell even deeper underground. Underland is a cheerless place where hunched gnomes are enslaved. Lit by a dull greenish light, the dark, calm waters of the Sunless Sea lead to a busy seaport where the Lady of the Green Kirtle has her castle. Once the Witch is destroyed, Narnians enjoy visiting the underground sea on hot summer days.

In contrast, the Land of Bism, the deepest level of Underland, is as bright as flame. A river of fire, with talking salamanders that look like miniature dragons, runs through this land. Precious gems such as diamonds and rubies are alive, growing like fruit.

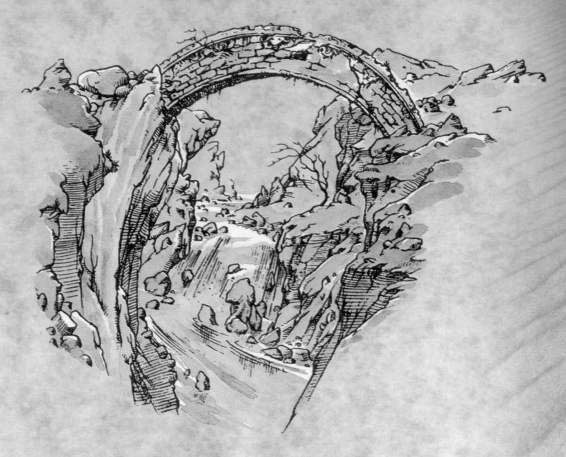

been cut off from the mainland and is now an island. It takes the children quite a while to realize this ruin is their former home and the wild orchards are the same apple trees they ordered planted when they were monarchs. Confirming their suspicions, they find the treasure room undisturbed. Fortunately, too, the apples are sweet and the water from the well remains pure. Cair Paravel is still protecting its rulers.

The meaning of the castle's name has been variously explained. But the most elegant explanation, offered by Martha Sammons in *A Guide Through Narnia*, is that the name is derived from the old British legal phrase "court paravail", meaning a lower or inferior court of law. Lewis seems to be implying that High Kings and Queens may

reign over Narnia from Cair Paravel, but their law will always be subject to Aslan's.

The Islands of the Eastern Sea

A King's Home at Sea

The *Dawn Treader* is King Caspian's ship, built much like an earthly galley. Made of wood, it has one large purple sail, green sides and its prow is shaped like the head of a dragon. When there is no wind or too much wind (during a storm), or when it is necessary to manoeuvre in port, the sail can be furled and thirty rowers using long oars take over. The ship can hold food and drink for up to twenty-eight days before it has to be restocked. To make the ship look more formidable, the crew hangs shields off the side of the boat, a tactic that Lewis

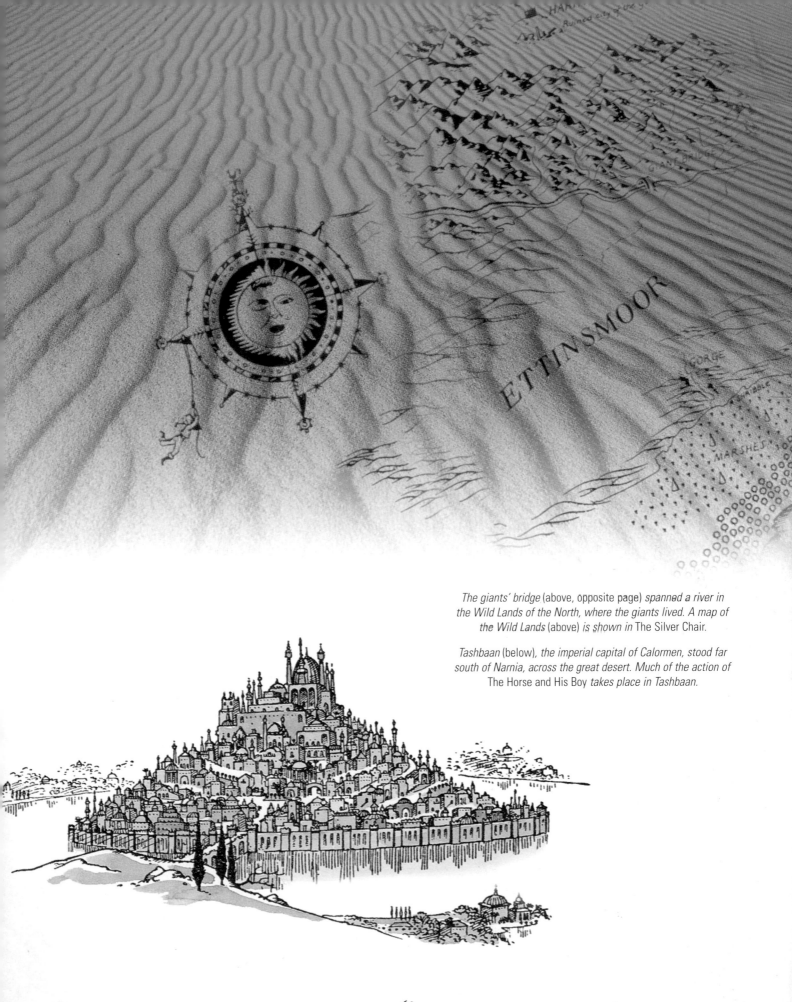

ETTINSMOOR

The giants' bridge (above, opposite page) *spanned a river in the Wild Lands of the North, where the giants lived. A map of the Wild Lands* (above) *is shown in* The Silver Chair.

Tashbaan (below), *the imperial capital of Calormen, stood far south of Narnia, across the great desert. Much of the action of* The Horse and His Boy *takes place in Tashbaan.*

borrowed from the Viking sailors. The ship's name comes from its duty—to head east, towards the dawn.

Lewis himself loved boats and gave Pauline Baynes a detailed description of the *Dawn Treader*. He wrote once of loving the taste of salt on his lips, and in *The Voyage of the* Dawn Treader, he imbues Edmund and, especially, Lucy with that love: ". . . when they . . . saw the whole western sky lit up with an immense crimson sunset, and felt the quiver of the ship, and tasted the salt on their lips, and thought of unknown lands on the Eastern rim of the world, Lucy felt that she was almost too happy to speak."

A group of three islands—**Felimath**, **Avra** and **Doorn**—make up the **Lone Islands**. They are far to the southeast of Cair Paravel. During the Golden Age of Narnia, these islands are happy places, but over the centuries they were slowly forgotten and fell into evil times. Historically, only sheep and shepherds have lived in the green val-

leys of Felimath, but Caspian and his fellow voyagers find that slave traders are using it as a base. On Doorn, the port town of Narrowhaven, with its white buildings, is the seat of the governor of the Lone Islands, who has become corrupt and profits from the slave trade. Avra, a pleasant green island, is home to Lord Bern, who lives at Bernstead, his grand estate there, and remains loyal to Caspian. Bern is one of the seven lords for whom Caspian is searching. Before continuing his voyage in search of the other six lords, Caspian deposes the wicked governor and names Bern the Duke of the Lone Islands.

South of the Lone Islands, **Dragon Island** is uninhabited but beautiful, with jagged cliffs, streams, wild goats and a bay. Here Eustace is separated from the rest, finds a dying dragon and the dragon's treasure and is turned into a dragon by his own greed, forcing the crew to camp out on the island until he is turned back into a boy.

The tiny **Burnt Island**, just to the east of Dragon Island, is dotted with the ruins of stone huts, soil blackened by recent fires, scattered bones and discarded weapons. "Pirates' work," says Caspian. Here, just before the *Dawn Treader* sails quickly away, Reepicheep finds the small boat that will take him to the End of the World.

Deathwater Island is another small island, with rugged terrain leading up to a steep hilltop. There are no people. At one end of the island is a small mountain lake, surrounded by cliffs. It is a beautiful sight, but the lake's water is cursed. Anything (or any*one*) who touches the water turns to gold. Any living thing dies, becoming a golden statue. A visitor who looks into the lake is suddenly struck with gold fever,

becoming greedy and thinking only about ways to use the water's power. Fortunately, the memory of the island is erased from the minds of the enchanted once they leave, if they are lucky enough to leave.

Nearly a month's sail east is a pristine island that is beautifully maintained, as if by English gardeners. **The Island of the**

In The Voyage of the *Dawn Treader, King Caspian sails his flagship, the dragon-prowed* Dawn Treader *(below)* across the Great Eastern Ocean. He and his companions visit the Lone Islands *(map opposite page),* heading ever eastward towards World's End. Along the way, they meet many strange creatures, including the one-legged Duffers *(opposite page),* also known as Dufflepuds or Monopods.

Duffers boasts a sandy beach, many well-trimmed trees, manicured lawns and one large, grey, ivy-covered house. The only inhabitants are the simpleminded Duffers and a magician named Coriakin, a star whose punishment is to maintain discipline among the Duffers. The Duffers, who are also known as Dufflepuds and Monopods, used to be small dwarfs, but, after the magician cast a spell on them, each now has only one leg and one big foot, so they are forced to hop. They were so unhappy with their appearance that they had their chief's young daughter, Clipsie, recite a spell to make them invisible. When the *Dawn Treader* finally arrives at the island, however, the Duffers are tired of invisibility. Lucy is the only one who has the power to make them visible again.

Darkness shrouds **Dark Island**. When the *Dawn Treader* approaches, a deep mist envelops the ship. The cloud has the power to make real dreams—not pleasant daydreams—come to life. The crew is trapped and terrified. Eventually Aslan guides the ship to safety and lifts the enchanted mist forever.

Ramandu's Island, with its gentle hills, is at the beginning of World's End. The sun here is much bigger and brighter, and a sweet smell pervades the land. A small valley leads to Aslan's table, which is filled each day with food for visitors who make it this far. Ramandu, a retired star, and his daughter guard the table and its three sleeping guests. It is also their job to protect the Stone Knife that was used by the White Witch to kill Aslan at the Stone Table.

The End

Two places in Narnia will always be synonymous with the end of Narnia itself, and the advent of an eternal world that Aslan

Then Aslan said, "Now make an end."

calls his own country or the "real Narnia". Here, one story ends, and another begins.

The **stable** is a small hut with a thatched roof. From the outside, it seems about twelve feet long and six feet wide. Located in Lantern Waste, it looks like any other stable. But when people go inside it in *The Last Battle*, they never come out. They wind up in different places, depending on how they have behaved in their lives. As

As Aslan is bringing old Narnia to an end in The Last Battle, *the sea rises and, with a great roaring noise, a towering wave of water submerges the entire world.*

King Tirian notes, "[T]he stable seen from within and the stable seen from without are two different places." For the friends of Narnia and all the good Narnian creatures, the stable door leads to a vast and vividly beautiful new world, Aslan's country, the real Narnia. But the Dwarfs who had turned against Aslan see only a dark, cold and cramped room.

Aslan's country is beyond World's End, after the Last Wave, in the utter East. When approaching Aslan's country by crossing the Eastern Sea, travellers find that the sea-water somehow becomes crystal-clear fresh water; drinking it makes them feel happy, alive and refreshed. Since the water is covered with white lilies, they name it the Silver Sea. In Aslan's country there is a high mountain range that is never covered in snow and the land is filled with orchards, waterfalls and meadows. The air is clearer here, and the blue sky comes down to the ground like a glass wall. It is always spring. Aslan's country is connected with all the other worlds in the universe but can only be reached by magic. Aslan ushers the friends of Narnia here at the end of *The Last Battle*, leading them through the stable. Once here, they discover that the Narnia they knew was nothing more than a "shadow" of Aslan's country. This is the real Narnia, where everything is bigger and brighter and clearer. Here old friends and loved ones are reunited, everybody is young again and all the friends of Narnia live forever with Aslan.

Getting There

...and Back

The rule is simple: Travelling to Narnia requires an invitation.

Certainly, there are exceptions, and many earthly people have travelled to Narnia accidentally through what Aslan calls "chinks or chasms between worlds". But such chinks are growing rarer, Aslan tells the Telmarines at the end of Prince Caspian, explaining how their ancestors fled into a cave on a South Pacific island and emerged on Narnia's world. That magical cave "was one of the last" of the chinks between worlds, Aslan says, although he adds, "I do not say the last."

It was, apparently, just such a combination of fate and magic that brought Digory

Travelling to Narnia by any means must have felt like stepping into a pristine and mysterious Earth. In the remote New Zealand outback, location scouts found enchanted landscapes (below) *where scenes were filmed for the movie of* The Lion, the Witch and the Wardrobe.

"You would not have called to me unless I had been calling to you," said the Lion.

and Polly to their first otherworldly destination in the Wood between the Worlds at the very beginning of *The Magician's Nephew*. Then the children simply chose a random pool to jump into as they attempted to elude the evil Jadis, and in this way they travelled to Narnia.

But under normal conditions, visitors must be called to Narnia. Even if it doesn't seem that way, they are pulled into Narnia only when needed. In *The Silver Chair*, Aslan tells Jill Pole that she and Eustace Scrubb must complete a task in Narnia. That is why "I called you and him here out of your own world," the Lion explains. Jill contradicts Aslan, saying, "[N]obody called me and Scrubb, you know. It was we who asked to come here." But Aslan replies, "You would not have called to me unless I had been calling to you."

Anyone who has visited Narnia is anxious to return. But it turns out that the traveller cannot control the voyage. In *The Lion, the Witch and the Wardrobe*, wise Professor Kirke (who once was young Digory) tells the Pevensies, "Yes, of course you'll get back to Narnia again someday. Once a King in Narnia, always a King in Narnia. But don't go trying to use the same route twice. Indeed, don't *try* to get there at all. It'll happen when you're not looking for it."

Each of the stories in *The Chronicles* introduces a new, unanticipated way to get to Narnia and a new way for the characters to return home again. These are the known ways of getting to Narnia and getting back again.

When Jill and Eustace are called to Narnia in The Silver Chair, *they arrive atop a cliff so high it cannot be compared with any cliff on Earth. But if it could, it might have been something like this dramatic cliff in New Zealand.*

The Magician's Nephew

The legendary island of Atlantis is lost to the seas of time and legend. But out of it came a small box. In that box is some dust from the Wood between the Worlds, a place with doorways to many other worlds. The box was given to Digory's uncle Andrew by Mrs Lefay, Andrew's godmother, who claimed to be descended from fairies. As Andrew told his nephew, "In fact, Digory, you are now talking to the last man (possibly) who really had a fairy godmother." From the dust, Uncle Andrew makes yellow and green rings. A yellow ring can transport a person out of this universe to the "in-between place" called the Wood between the Worlds. A green ring can take a traveller "out of the wood into a world"—any world. When someone wearing a green ring steps into one of the countless pools of water in the wood, the pool transports the ring wearer to another world.

First Polly and then Digory slip on the yellow rings, vanish from England and wind up in the Wood between the Worlds. Polly has the presence of mind to insist that they test the rings to be certain they can return home. When the test works, Polly next insists that they mark the pool that leads to Earth so they can find it again among the countless, identical pools in the wood. The children then travel to the dead city of Charn, back to England and finally to Narnia, which is just being created as they arrive.

When it is time to go home, Aslan tells them, "You need no rings when I am with you," and commands them to bury the rings for safe keeping. Digory and Polly look into the Lion's face and find themselves back in London, outside Digory's house.

The Lion, the Witch and the Wardrobe

As far as wardrobes go, the one in the spare room of the Professor's house is rather plain: large and wooden, with a long mirror on the

Digory and Polly first travelled to Narnia through a magic pond in the Wood between the Worlds (left).

The Pevensie children (opposite page, in a photo from the movie The Lion, the Witch and the Wardrobe) travel to and from Narnia through the wardrobe.

door. But it is made from the very special wood of a magical Narnian apple tree. When four siblings from London—Peter, Edmund, Susan and Lucy Pevensie—climb into the wardrobe and take a few steps, they find themselves in the snowy woods of Narnia.

After difficult quests, ferocious battles, dangerous encounters with evil magic and many other great adventures, they are crowned Narnia's High Kings and Queens and rule with justice and wisdom for many years. One day they chase a White Stag through the woods, pass the lamp-post in Lantern Waste and start to recall their old life on Earth. They keep walking and soon climb back through the wardrobe into the spare room of the Professor's house, at the same moment and the same place they had started out.

PRINCE CASPIAN

On her first trip to Narnia, Susan is given a magic horn which, when blown, always summons help. Susan leaves the horn in Narnia, and in a time of danger, Prince Caspian receives the treasured horn from his faithful teacher. In great need of aid, Caspian sounds the horn and summons the four children from Earth to Narnia. It happens to be at a moment when the Pevensies are sitting on a bench at the train station on their way back to boarding school. Suddenly they feel a tugging and are yanked from the bench right into the woods of Narnia.

"There were many chinks or chasms

Once they help Caspian gain his rightful throne and assure the return of the Old Ways, it is time to go home. Aslan orders a rough wooden frame to be set up in the woods. Built with three pieces of wood, "the whole thing looked like a doorway from nowhere into nowhere". But when the children step through it, they are back at the train station.

THE VOYAGE OF THE DAWN TREADER

Lucy and Edmund have the misfortune of having to spend the summer at their obnoxious cousin Eustace's house. One day, they are all in Lucy's bedroom looking at a painting of a ship on the wall when the ship suddenly begins to move. The three children are washed into the painting by a large wave and are suddenly swimming in the cold, salty water of Narnia's Great Eastern Sea next to King Caspian's ship, the *Dawn Treader*.

Following a long and adventurous voyage aboard the ship and on the islands, the children must go home. Aslan tears a hole in the blue sky, kisses them on their foreheads and sends them back to Lucy's room in Eustace's house.

between worlds in old times..."

THE SILVER CHAIR

Eustace is trying to cheer up his classmate Jill Pole, who is crying because the bullies at their school, Experiment House, won't leave her alone. Explaining why he has changed so dramatically since the last school term, Eustace tells Jill about his strange experiences in Narnia. Even though Jill doesn't quite believe Eustace's stories, she says she would like to go to Narnia. To avoid the bullies, they run through the schoolyard and discover that the door in a stone wall is unlocked. Passing through the doorway, they find themselves on a cliff high above Narnia.

When the time came for Earthlings to leave Narnia in Prince Caspian, *Aslan used three sticks to create a magical doorway between worlds. A Telmarine solider was the first to use the doorway (above left). In* The Voyage of the Dawn Treader *(above right), Eustace, Edmund and Lucy are pulled through a painting into Narnia's Great Eastern Ocean. They arrive dripping wet on the deck of King Caspian's ship.*

After they complete an important mission for Aslan, they follow him through the Narnian woods until they are suddenly back on the familiar school property on Earth, right in front of the stone wall again. But Aslan is with them and brings along King Caspian, who has been resurrected

from death by the Lion and appears to be a very young man. Aslan roars and the stone wall at Experiment House falls, revealing seven of the school bullies running to attack Jill and Eustace. But when the bullies see an enormous lion through the gap in the wall, they stop, terribly frightened. And the next thing they know, three armed figures in exquisite clothing—Caspian, Eustace and Jill—are beating them with a crop and the flats of swords. Aslan and Caspian, the only Narnian ever to visit Earth, remain on this world for only five minutes, but it is sufficient to change Experiment House and the bullies forever.

The Last Battle

Professor Digory Kirke has a feeling that something important is going to happen. He gathers all the children who have ever been to Narnia (except Susan, who has put Narnia behind her as a childish game) and invites them to dinner. Good King Tirian in Narnia appears, ghostlike, while they dine. The children know they need to find a way to get to Narnia to discover what the King needs.

They decide that Peter and Edmund must dig up the old rings that transported Digory and Polly to Narnia almost fifty years earlier. Peter and Edmund then will board a train from London while the other children board a train from the country. The plan is to meet at a station in the middle, near where Eustace and Jill go to school.

But before Edmund and Peter's train arrives for the transfer of the rings, Eustace and Jill find themselves jolted right out of their seats and into Narnia without needing the rings at all. As hard as they try, they cannot save the beloved land of Narnia from destruction. Aslan extinguishes Narnia's sun and brings the world's existence to a close. He explains that the old Narnia they all love is only a shadow of the real Narnia, where they will now live forever.

The doorway of the tiny stable in the Lantern Waste becomes a doorway to the real Narnia, and all those people and creatures who love Aslan and have stayed by his side are ushered into the new world that awaits them.

The children learn that the train Jill and Eustace were riding had crashed, as had the train that carried the other children and, coincidentally, their parents. So this time, there will be no trip back home to England; they are now in their only true home.

"So," said Peter, "night falls on Narnia."

It's About Time

One of the greatest intellectual revolutions in history took place in 1915, when Lewis was a seventeen-year-old student. Albert Einstein published a slim volume titled *Relativity: The Special and General Theory*. Einstein's theory of relativity, which had been partially released in 1905, proved that time, among other things, is not a universal constant. In his book, for instance, he demonstrated that a clock in motion "goes more slowly than when at rest". For the rest of his life, Lewis was intrigued by the idea that time could move at differing rates in different places. Nowhere is this fascination more evident than in *The Chronicles of Narnia*.

The passage of time in Narnia is completely independent of the passage of time on Earth. Thousands of years pass in Narnia in the course of the seven *Chronicles*. Whole civilizations rise and fall, land masses change shape, history turns into myth. On Earth though, only forty-nine years pass by. In *The Voyage of the* Dawn Treader, Lewis explains, "If you spent a hundred years in Narnia, you would still come back to our world at the very same hour of the very same day on which you left. And then, if you went back to Narnia after spending a week here, you might find that a thousand Narnian years had passed, or only a day, or no time at all. You never know till you get there." Is Narnia moving at the speed of light relative to Earth? Lewis never said, but after he finished the last book, he created a time line to track the comings and goings of the friends of Narnia alongside what was happening in Narnian history. The chart (next page), derived from Lewis's more elaborate time line, shows the major events in *The Chronicles* with the date they occurred in both Narnian and English time.

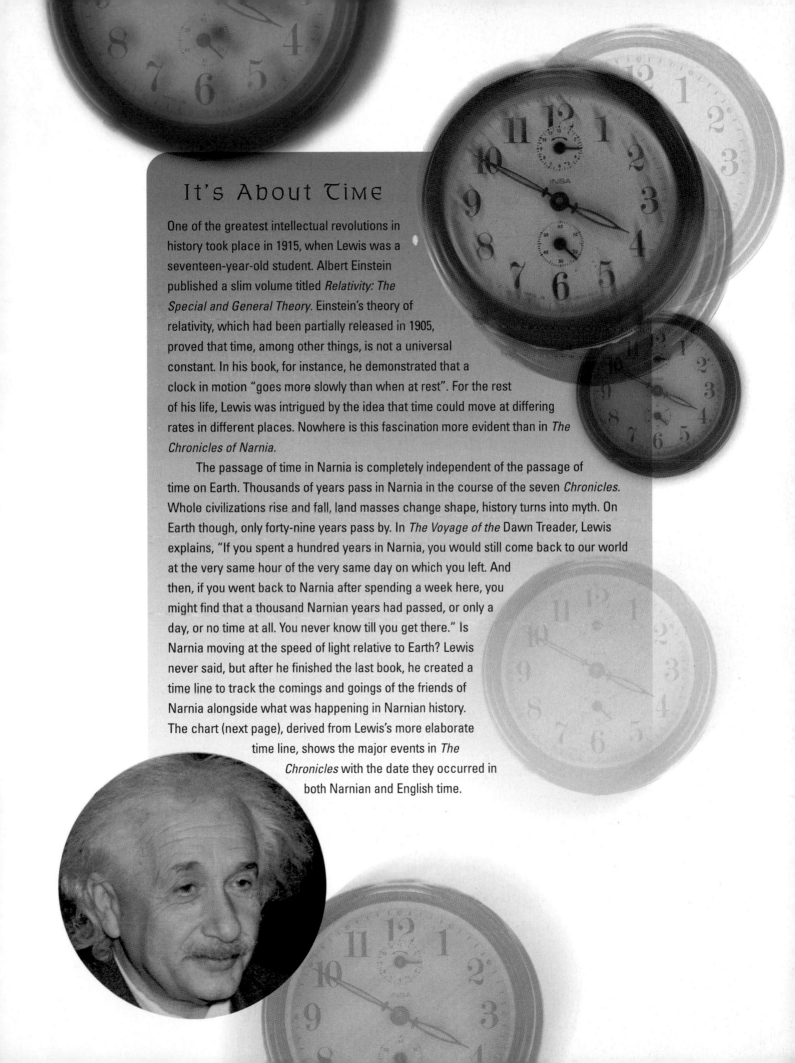

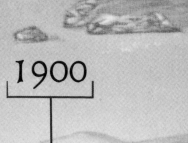

Digory and
Polly use
magic rings.

Peter, Susan,
Edmund and Lucy
Pevensie walk
through the
Professor's
wardrobe.

The endless winter
ends, and the
Golden Age of
Narnia begins.

Aslan sings Narnia
into existence.

1942

TIME

The friends of Narnia are in a serious train accident.

1949

The Pevensies are called back to Narnia to help Prince Caspian.

Eustace and Jill are brought into Narnia from their school.

Edmund, Lucy and Eustace are pulled through a painting to Caspian's ship.

Caspian is made King and the Old Ways are restored.

King Caspian journeys to the utter East.

Prince Rilian is rescued and the Lady of the Green Kirtle is vanquished.

The Last Battle between the Calormene and the Narnians. Aslan ushers in the end of Narnia.

2303   2306   2356   2555

TIME

Narnia's
Royal Visitors

⁓

WRITING fairy tales, Lewis felt, was often the best way to express what he wanted to say about the world. Using children as his protagonists, too, enabled him to better tell his tale. Just as Alice, after slipping down the rabbit hole,

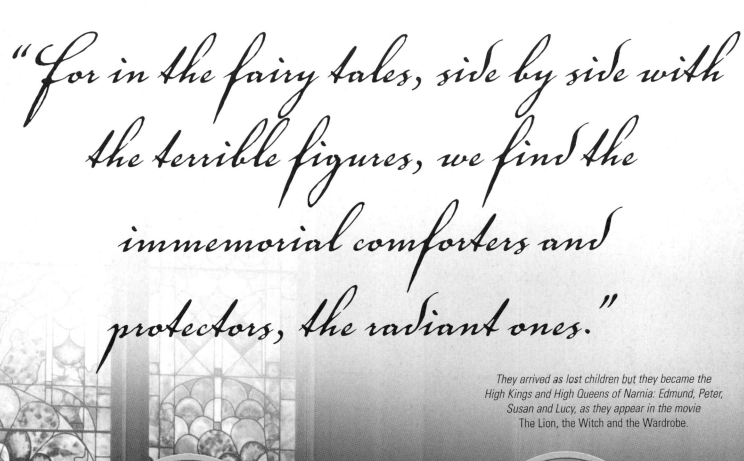

"For in the fairy tales, side by side with the terrible figures, we find the immemorial comforters and protectors, the radiant ones."

They arrived as lost children but they became the High Kings and High Queens of Narnia: Edmund, Peter, Susan and Lucy, as they appear in the movie The Lion, the Witch and the Wardrobe.

escorts readers through Wonderland with a perspective wholly influenced by her youth, so Lewis's travellers guide us through Narnia from a viewpoint accessible only to children.

Lewis's young travellers are still growing and changing, still unfamiliar with the ways of their own world, let alone a fantastical alternative one. Young readers, especially, recognize that these characters are no different from themselves: They make mistakes, get scared, are selfish, cranky and worse. But demanding circumstances—often involving life-or-death situations—bring out the best in Lewis's travellers. They

Digory Kirke and Polly Plummer (top) meet for the first time in The Magician's Nephew *when Digory scales the garden wall that separates his backyard from Polly's.*

Susan (bottom) *prepares to shoot an arrow as two of Narnia's exotic creatures watch in this scene from the movie* The Lion, the Witch and the Wardrobe.

find strength they didn't know they had and their innate goodness shines through in the end.

As Lewis scholar Clyde S. Kilby points out, "[I]n Narnia we are presented not so much with characters who are good or bad as with characters who are progressing toward one state or the other by their choices." Lewis felt that the people we meet in life are generally in this same state of change. In his book *The Weight of Glory*, he writes, "It is a serious thing to live in a society of possible gods and goddesses, to remember that the dullest and most uninteresting person you talk to may one day be a creature which, if you saw it now, you would be strongly tempted to worship, or else a horror and a corruption such as you now meet, if at all, only in a night-

mare. All day long we are, in some degree, helping each other to one or other of these destinations."

Douglas Gresham, Lewis's stepson, says Lewis developed this important idea after reading George MacDonald's allegorical fairy tale *The Princess and Curdie*, first published in 1882. In the MacDonald book, Curdie, a miner's son, is told by a magical princess that all men are either going up or going down—getting morally better or becoming worse. The manners and behaviour of two men may be exactly the same at some moment, but if one is getting better and the other is worsening, this "is just the greatest of all differences that could possibly exist between them", the princess tells Curdie. Thus, the princess cautions, many men are fated to spend their lives reverting to the base behaviour of beasts.

Lewis makes us care about Narnia by making us care about its people and creatures—both who and what they are and, even more, what they may become and the choices they make to get there.

The First Travellers

Digory Kirke, the first character we meet in *The Chronicles of Narnia*, is named after Lewis's beloved tutor, W. T. Kirkpatrick, but he seems to be modelled in part after Lewis himself. At twelve years old, Digory is sad

to great lengths to save his friend Polly and to rid London of the evil Witch, Jadis, who was set free by Digory's lack of self-discipline. Through Digory, Lewis illustrates the duality of good and bad that he observed in people with such stunning clarity.

Eventually, Digory manages to overcome his own strong emotions with his equally strong reasoning power and proves himself worthy to Aslan. He is rewarded with a

"Be winged. Be the father of all flying horses," roared Aslan...

because his father is away in India and his mother is very ill. In much the same way, young Jack Lewis had struggled at the age of nine with his mother's terminal cancer and his father's emotional distance.

Digory is no cardboard cutout boy; his character is complex and flawed, as are the characters of all real boys. His grief makes him impulsive at the beginning of *The Magician's Nephew*. He shows impatience, bad judgment and lack of foresight. But he changes with time. He goes

magic apple that saves his sick mother. He buries the apple core in his backyard and it grows and changes, much like Digory himself. The apple core becomes a tree and, years later, when a storm blows it down, Digory makes a wardrobe out of the wood. It is, of course, the magical wardrobe in *The Lion, the Witch and the Wardrobe*. It rests in the house of a wise Professor, who is none other than Digory grown up.

In *The Last Battle*, Digory's maturing is complete; he is a lord with a great beard who senses a time of need and gathers the friends of Narnia together at his home. The sad and impulsive young boy who was present at the creation of Narnia has become a wise and regal presence at its end.

Polly Plummer, age eleven, is Digory's London neighbour, living in the terraced house next door. With the exception of a guinea pig, she is the first to leave Earth, whisked unknowingly into the Wood between the Worlds. Polly has more common

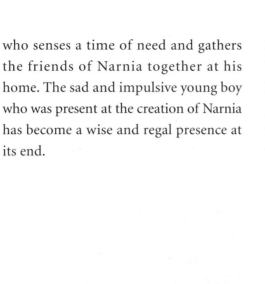

The hansom cab horse Strawberry is transformed by Aslan into Narnia's first flying horse and is given the name Fledge. Trying his new wings, Fledge takes Digory and Polly on a ride through the skies in The Magician's Nephew.

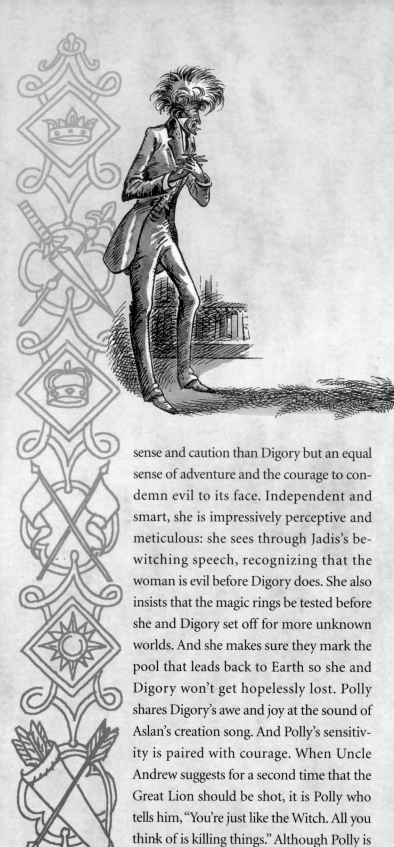

Digory's wicked uncle Andrew (left) *stands in his study in* The Magician's Nephew, *trying to explain Polly's sudden disappearance.*

What began with Andrew's magical experiments eventually leads, in The Lion, the Witch and the Wardrobe, *to the transformation of Peter Pevensie from an ordinary English schoolboy to a warrior king* (opposite page, in a concept drawing for the movie) *bearing Aslan's symbol on his chest, ready to do battle with the White Witch's army.*

sense and caution than Digory but an equal sense of adventure and the courage to condemn evil to its face. Independent and smart, she is impressively perceptive and meticulous: she sees through Jadis's bewitching speech, recognizing that the woman is evil before Digory does. She also insists that the magic rings be tested before she and Digory set off for more unknown worlds. And she makes sure they mark the pool that leads back to Earth so she and Digory won't get hopelessly lost. Polly shares Digory's awe and joy at the sound of Aslan's creation song. And Polly's sensitivity is paired with courage. When Uncle Andrew suggests for a second time that the Great Lion should be shot, it is Polly who tells him, "You're just like the Witch. All you think of is killing things." Although Polly is often frustrated with Digory, she remains a faithful and caring companion. She forgives him when he mistreats her and the

two remain lifelong friends, returning to Narnia at the end of *The Last Battle.*

Andrew Ketterley, Digory's wicked uncle Andrew, uses magic recklessly in his sadly bungled quest for power. He tricks Polly and Digory into being part of his experiment in magical travel and sends them off with no idea of what will become of them. For all the curiosity and determination he exhibits in working to become a magician, Andrew is weak, silly, vain and selfish. So consumed by his own needs and interests is he that when he does land in Narnia, he is too closed-minded to see its beauty and allure. Rather, he can't return home to London quickly enough. Later in *The Magician's Nephew*, Andrew is restrained from his wicked ways and becomes rather harmless.

Uncle Andrew claims **Mrs Lefay** as his godmother and tells Digory and Polly she

was one of the last on Earth to have fairy blood in her veins. Mrs Lefay, in all likelihood, is named after Morgan le Fay, the often wicked and scheming half-sister of King Arthur in the Arthurian legends, which Lewis loved. Given Mrs Lefay's connection to Atlantis and the sea, however, Lewis may have reached back further in time for this name to the Welsh sea goddess LeFay. If Mrs Lefay ever came close to Morgan's occasional wickedness, Lewis never tells us, noting only that she did "unwise things" for which she was jailed. On her deathbed, Mrs Lefay gave Andrew a box of magic dust from Atlantis. She must have known that Andrew couldn't be trusted, though, because she ordered him to destroy it. Instead, he keeps the dust and makes the rings that transport Digory and Polly into other worlds.

The Pevensie Children

The four Pevensie children are at the heart of *The Chronicles*. They appear, either together or in pairs, more often than any other characters except Aslan. And, of course, they are the High Kings and Queens of Narnia.

There has been speculation over the derivation of the surname Pevensie. The prevailing theory is that Lewis slightly altered the spelling of Pevensey Bay on the south coast of England, where William the Conqueror once landed and where a World War II base was located centuries later. By doing so,

Edmund Pevensie (opposite, in the movie *The Lion, the Witch and the Wardrobe*), creeps through the White Witch's eerie courtyard, which is filled with people and creatures she has turned to stone. Later, Edmund becomes a hero when he breaks the Witch's wand with his sword.

Lewis could also pay homage to the novel *Puck of Pook's Hill* by Rudyard Kipling, who was one of the writers he loved as a child. In that book a brother and sister live near a ruined castle named Pevensey, also on Pevensey Bay. They, too, were called "Son of Adam" and "Daughter of Eve". Coincidence? Not likely from the man who remembered everything he ever read.

Peter Pevensie, the oldest of the four siblings, is thirteen when we first meet him in *The Lion, the Witch and the Wardrobe*. He is a natural leader who looks after his younger siblings and tries to treat everyone fairly and with respect.

A brave fighter who becomes a great warrior, Peter first uses his sword and shield valiantly to rescue his sister Susan from the wolf Maugrim, head of the Witch's secret police. This earns him the name Sir Peter Wolf's-Bane. After his coronation, he is called King Peter the Magnificent, known for his courage, honesty and intelligence. As the High King, Peter has power over all the other kings that come after him. Peter's special position in Narnia is reflected at the conclusion of *The Last Battle*. After Father Time has sounded his horn to signal the end of the world, after the waters have risen and the sun has gone out, as a chill wind from a dead world turns everything to ice, Aslan gives Peter the honour of sealing off the dead Narnian world from the real Narnia. " 'Peter, High King of Narnia,' said Aslan. 'Shut the Door.' " And Peter pulls the door closed and locks it with a golden key.

Susan Pevensie is twelve when she is introduced, a year younger than her brother Peter.

Edmund lies and risks his siblings' safety to get the Turkish Delight from the White Witch.

After a long separation, Lucy (below) *finds Aslan in the Narnian woods and rushes to embrace him in* Prince Caspian.

Father Christmas (opposite page) *as he looks in the movie* The Lion, the Witch and the Wardrobe.

Like him, she looks out for her younger siblings, although her style is less to their liking: She is bossy. She is also a bit overconcerned with being grown-up and, perhaps as a consequence, less taken with Narnia than her siblings. In *Prince Caspian*, for instance, Susan pretends not to believe that Lucy saw Aslan because she doesn't want to have to take a more arduous trip. She feels guilty, though, and apologizes to Lucy. Her bow and arrows inspire her to become an expert archer, and she fights alongside her brothers in one battle. Known as Queen Susan the Gentle, she is kind and a good swimmer and grows up to be very beautiful. In *The Last Battle*, Lewis tells us that Susan is no longer a friend of Narnia; she no longer believes in it. She is left alive on Earth, while the rest of her family is killed in a train accident and transported to Aslan's country.

When Lewis first introduces him, ten-year-old **Edmund Pevensie** is *not* a nice person. Never a fan of the boarding school system, Lewis paints Edmund as an unpleasant example of how boys quickly learn to pick on other boys in this environment. When Edmund returns home from school, he picks on his younger sister, Lucy, and is willing to lie and risk his siblings' safety to get the sweets he wants from the White Witch. After he comes to his senses and realizes the Witch is evil, Edmund—with Aslan's help—finds the strength to change his ways. It is his bravery and quick thinking that turns the tide

Finally, Christmas!

A pivotal scene in *The Chronicles* occurs in *The Lion, the Witch and the Wardrobe* when three of the Pevensie children (along with Mr and Mrs Beaver, who are guiding them to Aslan) receive special gifts from Father Christmas. His sudden and unexpected appearance in Narnia is an important sign that the Witch's evil power is waning. Her subjugation of Narnia had been marked by a century of unrelieved winter. As Mr. Beaver explains, the Witch "made it always winter and never Christmas". So the arrival of Father Christmas is the first significant sign in a hundred years that good is triumphing.

The gifts Father Christmas gives to three of the Pevensie children are both a reflection of each child's developing personality and a portent of the destiny awaiting each.

For Peter, Father Christmas has "tools not toys". He gives Peter, the future High King and war leader, a silver-coloured shield emblazoned with the sign of Aslan—"a red lion, as bright as a ripe strawberry at the moment when you pick it." Peter also accepts a gold-hilted sword, just the right size for a boy his age, along with a sheath and sword belt.

Susan receives a quiver of arrows and a bow. "It does not easily miss," Father Christmas says. But the gift that will turn the tide in one of Narnia's darkest hours is a little horn that summons help when it is sounded. This is the horn that will summon the children to Narnia's aid when the wicked Lord Protector Miraz is threatening to wipe out the Old Narnians in *Prince Caspian*.

Lucy, the youngest, is given a crystal vial with a powerful healing potion made from "the juice of one of the fire-flowers that grow in the mountains of the sun". She also gets a "dagger to defend yourself at great need". These are portentous gifts for the child who will valiantly work to heal divisions and keep her brothers and sister united in the face of danger and uncertainty.

For poor Edmund, who has betrayed his siblings and is with the White Witch at the moment of the gift giving, there is nothing. Edmund, it seems, will have to make his own way to his destiny without the help of special gifts.

But What About Susan?

At the end of *The Last Battle*, all the friends of Narnia are invited to live in Aslan's country, the real Narnia, forever—except Susan. When she grows up back on Earth, Susan's memories of Narnia become dim and she eventually believes their adventures were just games they made up. She loses sight of all the things they learned as Kings and Queens. According to Jill Pole in *The Last Battle*, "She's interested in nothing nowadays except nylons and lipstick and invitations. She always was a jolly sight too keen on being grown-up." Aslan's country is for people who believe in the goodness of Narnia and have joy in their hearts, and Susan had turned away from it to pursue more mundane activities.

For decades, children have bemoaned poor Susan's fate. Being denied entrance to the glorious place called Aslan's country, or the real Narnia, seems a devastating end. But Lewis pointed out in a letter he wrote to a boy in 1957 that it's not necessarily the end for Susan: "The books don't tell us what happened to Susan. She is left alive in this world at the end, having by then turned into a rather silly, conceited young woman. But there is plenty of time for her to mend, and perhaps she will get to Aslan's country in the end—in her own way."

in the big battle with the Witch in *The Lion, the Witch and the Wardrobe*, and he becomes known as King Edmund the Just. Along with Lucy, Edmund appears in the most books in *The Chronicles*.

Lucy Pevensie, only eight when she is sent to the Professor's house, is the first of her sib-lings to enter Narnia. As the most sensitive and thoughtful, as well as the youngest, Lucy is the most in tune with the fantastical world and the creatures in it. She sees Aslan more often than the others do, and she under-stands him better. She is loving and insight-ful and has a great sense of adventure. While Lucy is sometimes dismissed because of her

Lewis wrote that Eustace Clarence Scrubb almost deserved his name.

Susan (opposite page) *holds up a chessman of pure gold that she has found near a well in* Prince Caspian. *It is the children's final clue that they have returned to Cair Paravel, now in ruins after hundreds of Narnian years.*

In The Voyage of the *Dawn Treader, Eustace* (right) *shows what a nasty, foolish boy he is by grabbing Reepicheep's tail and twirling the valiant mouse around and around.*

youth, she is often put in the position of having to convince the others of what direction to take—and does so admirably. In fact, she is called Queen Lucy the Valiant because she will stand up to any foe, large or small. Lucy uses her vial of healing potion first to cure Edmund after he is seriously wounded in the big battle at the Fords of Beruna. Lucy is probably named after Lewis's goddaughter Lucy Barfield, to whom *The Lion, the Witch and the Wardrobe* is dedicated. Of her godfather, the real Lucy said in later years, "I think he must have understood me right from the start. He was a marvellous man."

MORE TRAVELLERS

Lewis wrote that **Eustace Clarence Scrubb** almost deserved his name, which gives a clear indication of the Pevensie cousin's unpleasant personality. At nine years of age in *The Voyage of the* Dawn Treader, Eustace is surly and disagreeable and a bully. Worst of all, as Lewis points out, he has no imagination. From the start, he hates being stuck in Narnia and wants to go home. As with many of Lewis's young characters, though, transformation is possible for Eustace. After he is unwittingly turned into a dragon, he finally understands the need for friendship and becomes a much nicer person (although he still complains occasionally). Later on Earth, at Experiment House, he shows real concern

93

for Jill, who is being pursued by the school bullies. When he is sent back to Narnia in *The Silver Chair*, and later in *The Last Battle*, Eustace proves himself a loyal, brave and capable boy.

Jill Pole is a classmate of Eustace and hates Experiment House even more than he does. While she is a smart girl, Jill is very angry and a bit stuck-up when we meet her in *The Silver Chair*. During her time in Narnia, she is humbled and grows to be more understand-

and she's a housewife. Frank is pulled into Narnia, along with his horse, Strawberry, when they both get tangled up with Digory and Jadis on the streets of London in *The Magician's Nephew*. Frank has a kind nature and an open heart, and Aslan chooses him to be the first King of Narnia. When Aslan asks Frank if he would like to live in Narnia "always", the cabby answers, "If my wife was here neither of us would ever want to go back to London, I reckon." So Aslan calls Helen from Earth, and she and Frank rule

Frank and Helen rule Narnia...

ing. She also bravely plays her part in rescuing Prince Rilian. In *The Last Battle*, when she is a few years older, Jill's bravery and quick thinking go a long way towards helping the King fight the ultimately losing battle. Lewis may have taken the name Jill from one of the students who stayed with him during the air raids of World War II, Jill Flewett. That Jill grew up to be an actress and married the grandson of Sigmund Freud. She and Lewis kept in touch for many years.

Unlike most of Lewis's other heroic travellers, **Frank** and **Helen** are not children, but they possess a humility and good-hearted openness that is almost childlike. In London, Frank and Helen are regular folk—he's a cabby who drives a horse-drawn carriage

Narnia with grace and kindness. Their descendants become Kings not only of Narnia, but of Archenland to the south and the isles of the Great Eastern Ocean.

Strawberry is the lone animal that travels from Earth to Narnia in *The Chronicles*, and his transformation is the most profound. Tired and mistreated by Jadis in London, Strawberry is ever more refreshed as he moves into the fantastical world. When the animals are given the ability to talk at the creation of Narnia, Strawberry becomes first a Talking Horse and then one with wings who goes by the name **Fledge**. Fledge offers to fly Digory and Polly on a very important journey, and he also returns with Frank and Helen in *The Last Battle*.

The Golden Age of Narnia

The Pevensie siblings have the distinct honour of being the High Kings and Queens of Narnia. Some or all of them appear in five of the seven books, and they are famous throughout Narnian history for their great deeds. When they are first crowned, Aslan tells them, "Once a king or queen in Narnia, always a king or queen. Bear it well, Sons of Adam! Bear it well, Daughters of Eve." They take this responsibility very seriously.

When the Pevensies sit on the four thrones in the Great Hall at Cair Paravel, Narnia enters its Golden Age. As the High King, Peter becomes skilled in battle. Edmund can be counted on to give valuable, sound advice to anyone who needs help, and Susan and Lucy are much beloved for their kind and gentle natures. During their reign, they make sure that Narnia's enemies do not harm the land or its inhabitants, the Talking Animals are given freedom again to live as they please, and the giants to the north are driven back. All remnants of the White Witch's evil army are eventually destroyed, an attack from Calormen is staved off, and an era of peace is ushered in. For fifteen "golden" years, the Pevensies rule over a happy land.

Upon their return to Earth after this time, though, the Pevensies find they have not aged at all. Many readers thought it was strange that the Pevensies grew up in Narnia and then got younger again back on Earth. In a letter to a young girl in 1953, Lewis responded to this concern: "I feel sure *I'm* right to make them grow up in Narnia. Of course they will grow up in this world too. You'll see. You see, I don't think age matters so much as people think. Parts of me are still 12 and I think other parts were already 50 when I was 12; so I don't feel it v.[ery] odd that they grow up in Narnia while they are children in England."

The four thrones in the Great Hall at Cair Paravel (below, from the Disney-Walden Media movie The Lion, the Witch and the Wardrobe) are the symbol of Narnia's Golden Age.

The
People and
Creatures
of Narnia

—

enneth Tynan, the British drama critic, theatre historian and playwright, used to play a rather odd game with his old Oxford tutor, C. S. Lewis. Lewis asked Tynan to pick a number from one to forty to identify a bookshelf in Lewis's sitting room at Magdalen College. Another number from one to twenty would select a book on that shelf. In similar fashion, Tynan was required to pick a random page and then a line on the page, which he read aloud. Lewis then immediately named

Ancient History (or, The Mythology of Narnia)

Myths, C. S. Lewis wrote in his 1960 book *Miracles,* are a "real though unfocused gleam of divine truth falling on human imagination".

Lewis had a lifelong fascination with classical Egyptian mythology, Greek and Roman myths, Norse fables, medieval legends and European fairy tales. Lewis's wide-ranging love of myths is evident in the vast assortment of creatures that populate the land of Narnia. The whole series, Lewis said, began with the image of a Faun, a Roman mythological figure who is half man and half goat.

Some creatures are presented with the traits they possess in classical literature. Bacchus, the Greek god of wine, is so true to his original nature that his wildness makes the Pevensie girls uncomfortable. But not all the creatures in Narnia are as true to their origins. The original Roman Fauns, for example, were Bacchus's nymph-chasing drinking companions, but Mr Tumnus seems far more timid and certainly better mannered.

Many of the creatures—such as Dwarfs, Unicorns, dragons, werewolves and even Father Christmas—have a long history in European folklore. Echoing the great legends of King Arthur, the values of chivalry and devotion to a sacred quest are found in Reepicheep, the brave leader of the talking Mice. Reepicheep seeks a place he has longed for his whole life: the End of the World. In *The Voyage of the* Dawn Treader, as he sails off to the utter East, his final destination, he throws his sword into the sea and it stands upright, its hilt above the surface, just as King Arthur's sword once stood in the stone.

A lover of Norse myth and the Nordic world, Lewis added many Norse touches to *The Chronicles.* To end the world, the watchman of the Norse gods blows a sacred horn, much as Father Time blows the horn to herald the end of Narnia. And the *Dawn Treader* resembles a Viking ship, with its single sail, rows of oars and dragon figurehead. Like the Viking explorers, too, Caspian scares away his enemies by hanging shields along the side of his ship to make it seem more warlike.

Lewis did not feel constrained by one tradition or another, often mixing a few together, sometimes even in the same scene. When Jadis tempts Digory to eat the forbidden apple, for instance, she is like the serpent in Genesis tempting Eve to eat the apple in the Garden of Eden. Yet the apple's healing effect on Digory's mother hearkens to stories of Norse gods staying youthful and healthy by eating magical apples. It is this type of combining of mythologies that Lewis's good friend J. R. R. Tolkien complained of, but Lewis had a story to tell, and he told it using all the material at his command.

the book and discussed the material on that particular page.

Tynan's story is told by another famous student of Lewis's, Alastair Fowler, the pre-eminent scholar of English literature. Remembering Lewis fondly in a *Yale Review* article, Fowler wrote, "Tynan's anecdote usefully suggests the sort of memory involved; not memory by rote (although Lewis had plenty of that) but…memory of the substance, aimed at grasp of contents through their structure."

As the game demonstrated, Lewis was a reader with a memory well matched to his appetite for ideas. He was steeped in classical mythologies and philosophies, as well as less ancient texts in English and other modern languages. His extraordinarily sharp memory, honed by years of drawing together quotations and ideas for debates and lectures, retained the substance of virtually everything he read.

When he populated Narnia, Lewis dug deeply into his vast reserve of knowledge to create characters based on archetypes, mythologies, folktales and the wellspring of his own imagination. As a result, Narnia's inhabitants are a diverse bestiary from a dazzling array of cultural traditions and historical periods. The people and creatures of Narnia include an all-powerful Lion, as well as brave and chivalrous Mice. There are pagan mythological creatures from Centaurs

King Caspian the Tenth's dragon-prowed Dawn Treader (opposite), with its single sail and many oars, greatly resembled ancient Viking ships (right) from Earth.

Aslan is living proof that a thing can be "good and terrible at the same time".

to Satyrs to Fauns, alongside Christian figures like Father Christmas and unique inventions like the pessimistic, web-footed Marsh-wiggles. There are characters from relatively modern folktales, such as Giants and Dwarfs. Figures from medieval history—human Kings, Queens, Princes and lords—share the page with the ancient persona of a beautiful woman who is the quintessence of evil. Armies are populated by eagles and owls who soar through the skies and Earthmen who live deep underground. Creatures walk on two legs, run on four or even hop along on one. And presiding over this amazing cast is an awesome, magical Lion, huge and powerful yet loving and gentle, whose golden mane is wondrous and whose roar can shake the earth.

Lewis's beautifully detailed and various creations include supremely good characters, purely evil ones and many in between. Some are loved, others hated and some simply are intended to be comical. But they all have one thing in common: They are unforgettable, even by those who do not possess C. S. Lewis's celebrated memory.

The Greatest Hero

Aslan reigns over everything and everyone in Narnia.

The Great Lion created Narnia and he protects it with a fierce and constant love. The son of the "Emperor-over-the-Sea", he is king of beasts, the highest king among all kings and the powerful embodiment of pure goodness. He is loved by the good creatures of Narnia, by the Pevensie children and by the other earthly visitors (except wicked Uncle Andrew). He is hated by those who are evil or simply misguided. But his majestic presence inspires a reverential fear in virtually everyone, good or wicked. Aslan is living proof that a thing can be "good and terrible at the same time", as Lewis writes, describing the Pevensies' first meeting with the Great Lion in *The Lion, the Witch and the Wardrobe*. "For when they tried to look at Aslan's face they just caught a glimpse of the golden mane and the great, royal, solemn, overwhelming eyes; and then they found they couldn't look at him and went all trembly." Aslan is awesome in the truest sense of the word.

In appearance, the Lion is many things. His gaze is regal, powerful, terrifying and compassionate all at once. His build is powerful; his coat a "soft roughness of golden fur" . Most intriguing, Aslan appears to be different sizes in different situations and to different people. He can be as large as an ordinary lion or a horse or a young elephant. Sometimes his colour is brighter than at other times; his fur can appear yellow or gold. In some respects, Aslan becomes whatever the onlooker needs to see at that time.

In *The Lion, the Witch and the Wardrobe*, Mr Beaver and the Pevensie children discuss the Great Lion:

". . . if there's anyone who can appear before Aslan without their knees knocking, they're either braver than most or else just silly."

"Then he isn't safe?" said Lucy.

"Safe?" said Mr Beaver; "don't you hear what Mrs Beaver tells you? Who said anything about safe? 'Course he isn't safe. But he's good. He's the King, I tell you."

"I'm longing to see him," said Peter, "even if I do feel frightened when it comes to the point."

In *Prince Caspian*, Lucy sees Aslan for the first time in many years. She believes the Lion has changed, but Aslan explains it is really Lucy who is different:

"Welcome, child," he said.

"Aslan," said Lucy, "you're bigger."

"That is because you are older, little one," answered he.

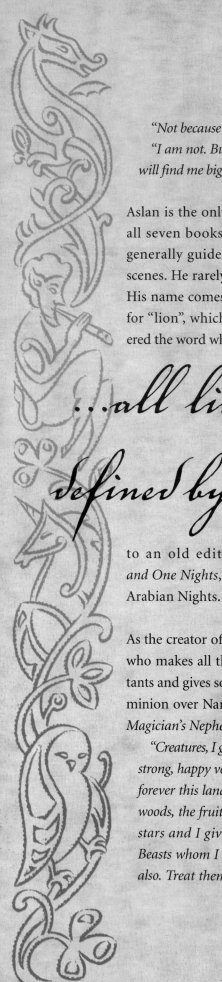

"Not because you are?"

"I am not. But every year you grow, you will find me bigger."

Aslan is the only character to appear in all seven books of *The Chronicles* and generally guides the action behind the scenes. He rarely is seen in Narnia itself. His name comes from the Turkish word for "lion", which is *aslan*. Lewis discovered the word while reading the footnotes

but do not go back to their ways lest you cease to be Talking Beasts."

Lewis gave Aslan both an aura of brightness and a special smell. In *The Horse and His Boy*, the boy Shasta experiences both when he meets Aslan for the first time. "The High King above all kings stooped toward him. Its mane, and some strange and solemn perfume that hung about the mane, was all round him. It touched his forehead with its

...all living things in Narnia...are defined by their relationship to Aslan.

to an old edition of *The Thousand and One Nights*, otherwise known as the Arabian Nights.

As the creator of Narnia, Aslan is the one who makes all the world's other inhabitants and gives some both speech and dominion over Narnia, as recounted in *The Magician's Nephew*:

"Creatures, I give you yourselves," said the strong, happy voice of Aslan. "I give to you forever this land of Narnia. I give you the woods, the fruits, the rivers. I give you the stars and I give you myself. The Dumb Beasts whom I have not chosen are yours also. Treat them gently and cherish them

tongue. He lifted his face and their eyes met. Then instantly the pale brightness of the mist and the fiery brightness of the Lion rolled themselves together into a swirling glory and gathered themselves up and disappeared."

Aslan can take the form of other animals. As a domestic cat in *The Horse and His Boy*, he keeps Shasta company during a long night in the desert, and as a lamb in *The Voyage of the* Dawn Treader, he welcomes the children to the shores at World's End.

Aslan is often cryptic in his instructions, leaving the children to make their own decisions—and their own mistakes. But he is

never far away when they are in serious trouble. In *The Last Battle*, each creature and person must make a final reckoning to Aslan. The Lion looks into their eyes to see if they return the gaze with love or with hate, and he determines their fate accordingly.

Peter (right, in the movie *The Lion, the Witch and the Wardrobe*) becomes the leader of the Narnian forces who are allied with Aslan.

As *The Chronicles* unfold, it soon becomes clear that all living things in Narnia, from the lowliest tree to High King Peter, are defined by their relationship to Aslan. They are divided into just two categories—those who are loyal to Aslan, and those who serve other masters or only themselves. According to their stance for or against Aslan, they are, essentially, either heroes or villains in the great, eternal tale of Narnia.

HEROES

Aravis is a wealthy teenager, the only daughter of Calormene nobleman Kidrash Tarkaan. Her mother is dead and her cruel stepmother arranges for her to marry a much older man who is a loathsome, social-climbing bureaucrat in Calormen's evil government. Aravis, an accomplished horsewoman, escapes this unacceptable marriage by running away with the horse Hwin. But unbeknownst to Aravis, Hwin is a Narnian horse who can talk. At first, Aravis is nothing more than a product of her aristocratic, Calormene upbringing—conceited, self-centred and superior. Thinking that the boy

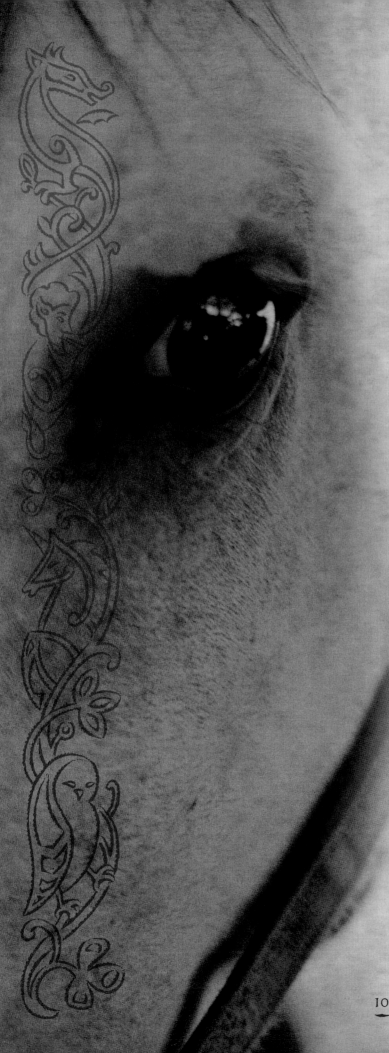

Shasta is a commoner and a horse thief, she treats him with contempt. But her experiences with Shasta and the talking horses teach her much about the inner worth of all beings. As they flee north, seeking freedom, Aravis learns humility and the importance of friendship. She plays an integral role in saving Narnia by warning her companions of the danger to Archenland from a Calormene attack. And when she grows up, Aravis and Shasta, now revealed to be the king's long-lost son Prince Cor, marry. Eventually, they rule over Archenland, the new queen's adopted land.

The **Beavers** are warm, trustworthy, hardworking creatures who love their home and peace. They take in the four Pevensies when they arrive in Narnia, even though they, too, fear the White Witch's wrath. They tell the children all about Aslan and the Witch and the endless winter her magic has brought to the land. Mr and Mrs Beaver take Peter, Susan and Lucy to meet the Lion. The Beavers' willingness to endanger their own lives to help the children makes them all lifelong friends and allies.

Bree and **Hwin** are Narnian horses who were both captured at an early age and forced to serve masters in Calormen. As Narnian beasts, they can talk, but they both hide that talent during their servitude in Calormen for

Bree (left), *a talking Narnian horse, is a central character in* The Horse and His Boy.

Peter, Lucy and Susan (opposite, in a scene from the movie *The Lion, the Witch and the Wardrobe*), *enjoy the warmth of Mr and Mrs Beaver's home, where they are treated to a dinner of potatoes and fish.*

Lucy thought the Beavers had a very snug little home....

fear of what would be done to them. Bree, whose full name is Breehy-hinny-brinny-hoohy-hah, is a proud and vain warhorse when he first meets young Shasta, but as their adventures continue, he learns humility and becomes aware of others' feelings and needs. Hwin is initially a shy horse, but more than once it is her good judgment that saves the journey. One of the central themes of *The Horse and His Boy* is Bree's journey, not just across the desert but from a doubter to a believer. Initially, Bree cannot believe that Aslan really exists. But when Bree encounters the Great Lion face-to-face, he is converted to believing in Aslan and admits to having been foolish. His triumph over his own pride and his discovery of the truth mark one of the crucial transformations of *The Chronicles*.

Caspian the Tenth is one embodiment in *The Chronicles* of the power of loyalty, humility and persistence to change history. Caspian, first as a young prince and later as king, plays an important part in the history of Narnia, even though he sometimes plays it reluctantly. Raised by his evil uncle Miraz after his father's murder, Caspian manages to remain loyal both to his father's memory and to the old ways of Narnia. Even though Miraz despises Aslan and has chased many of Narnia's oldest inhabitants into hiding, Caspian holds on to the Narnian values of loving Aslan and respecting the Talking Animals, the Dwarfs and the others who are the Old Narnians. He finds the strength to leave behind everything he's ever known in order

Caspian…knew that he had escaped death by an inch.

Caspian (opposite, below) *races to escape from his evil uncle in* Prince Caspian.

Farsight the eagle (right) *is a loyal counsellor to King Tirian in* The Last Battle.

to fight on behalf of the Old Narnians. After calling for help with Susan's magic horn, he is aided by Aslan and the Pevensies in defeating his uncle and restoring the old ways. Three years later, Caspian sets out on the *Dawn Treader* in search of the utter East and the seven loyal lords whom his uncle had banished. When Caspian achieves his goals, he tries to abdicate the throne so he may continue with Reepicheep to Aslan's country. But he sadly agrees to abandon the quest and remain King after the children remind him of his duty to Narnia and Aslan speaks to him through a golden lion's head that hangs in his cabin. Caspian, as he had promised, goes on to marry the daughter of Ramandu, a retired star, and rules well for many years. When he eventually dies of old age, he dies happy, knowing that his son, Rilian, has been returned to Narnia from his captivity in Underland. One of the King's few regrets in life was that he never was able to visit Earth. But at the end of *The Silver Chair*, Aslan brings Caspian back to life, makes him young again and grants his wish. The Lion allows the newly revived King to spend five minutes on Earth before going on to his final destination, Aslan's country.

Doctor Cornelius, Caspian's beloved tutor in *Prince Caspian*, appears to be a wise, mild-mannered academic but is actually a valiant revolutionary. Cornelius secretly wants to overthrow wicked King Miraz, Caspian's uncle, in order to preserve the old ways and make Caspian the king. Small and fat with a long, silvery beard, Cornelius looks "very wise, very ugly, and very kind". He is actually half Dwarf, but he has to hide it because Miraz has banned all the Old Narnians—the mythic creatures and Talking Beasts. Doctor Cornelius bravely defies Miraz's direct orders and teaches Caspian the true history of Narnia. When he learns Caspian's uncle is planning to kill Caspian, the tutor arranges the young prince's escape.

Farsight the Eagle stays with the brave Centaur Roonwit during his last hour of life and

carries to King Tirian the Centaur's final, prophetic words "to remember that all worlds draw to an end and that noble death is a treasure which no one is too poor to buy". Farsight also delivers the news to Tirian that Cair Paravel has been captured. Upon hearing Farsight's messages, Tirian proclaims that "Narnia is no more". Farsight's name seems

he also uses the little-known term for a group or flock of owls, which is a "parliament".) When Glimfeather first appears, he seems a bit befuddled and comical. Like his fellow owls, he speaks partly in rhyme. "Whoo! Tu-whoo! What a to-do! I can't think clearly yet. It's too early," he tells Eustace and Jill. But after nightfall, the nocturnal owl is very busi-

Puddleglum's faith breaks the Queen of Underland's enchantment....

to honour the fact that he has "the best eyes of all living things"—eyes that can see great distances and also peer into men's souls. It is Farsight who sees that the leader of the Calormenes, Rishda Tarkaan, is a hypocrite who, as Farsight realizes, "has called on gods he does not believe in." Farsight fights valiantly in battle, and when he, too, is killed, he is given a special place in the real Narnia, flying above the Earth children.

Glimfeather is an enormous, white-feathered Talking Owl, as tall as a "good-sized dwarf", who flies Jill Pole to the parliament of owls in *The Silver Chair*. (In giving the owls a parliamentary organization, Lewis seems to offer a humorous poke at "The Parliament of Fowls", a poem by Geoffrey Chaucer. But

nesslike, issuing instructions to the children that he clearly expects to be obeyed. He also proves to be honest, blunt and loyal to the king, all of which prove important in helping the children to execute the mission that Aslan has set for them: find the missing Prince Rilian.

Good Giants of Narnia are few in number but make up for it in the greatness of their hearts. **Rumblebuffin** is an enemy of the White Witch—she turned him to stone in her courtyard, where he was trapped until Aslan breathed on his feet, bringing the giant back to life. Rumblebuffin then gladly helps Aslan and the other revived creatures escape the Witch's courtyard by breaking down the gate, two towers and part of the encircling wall with his club. He is rewarded by the Pevensies when they become the Kings and Queens of Narnia. Like most giants, Rumblebuffin is not very smart, but he comes from a good family, is extremely polite and respects the rights of "little 'uns", as he calls normal-sized beings. He is so tall that he finds it difficult to hear people talking to him, so instructions often must be repeated.

Jewel, a white Unicorn with a blue horn, is King Tirian's best friend. He never doubts Aslan's existence, and always has an intelligent and noble thought to share. A fierce warrior, he is killed in the final battle and is taken to the real Narnia.

Puddleglum the Marsh-wiggle has a tall, skinny body, webbed hands and feet like a frog and "greeny-grey" hair, the strands of which are more like reeds than human hair. Marsh-wiggles are one with the watery, reedy, muddy marshes north of Cair Paravel where they live in wigwams and fish for eels with long poles and lines. They are as fond of their privacy as eel stew. After dinner, they like to smoke pipes filled with heavy, muddy tobacco. Puddleglum, like all Marsh-wiggles, is philosophical and pessimistic, always expecting the worst. Although he serves as the book's comic relief, he is also brave and has good sense, which is why he is chosen to assist Eustace and Jill in their quest to save Prince Rilian. More importantly, Puddleglum possesses unshakeable faith in the power of good. He is prepared to

believe in goodness whether it exists or not, simply because it is the right thing in which to believe. It is Puddleglum's faith that breaks the Queen of Underland's enchantment of him and his companions, making it possible for them to rescue Prince Rilian and return to the world's surface. As Lewis's stepson Douglas Gresham reports: "Many of the characters [in Narnia] were drawn from people living in and around The Kilns [Lewis's longtime home]. The classic example of this is Puddleglum the Marsh-wiggle, a direct modelling of our gardener, Fred Paxford." In his book *Lenten Lands*, Gresham recounts a conversation with Paxford to illustrate the gardener's somewhat pessimistic outlook: " 'Good morning, Fred,' I might say.

The large white owl Glimfeather (below) manages to be comical, befuddled, wise and businesslike in The Silver Chair.

'Ah, looks loike rain afore lunch though, if'n it doan't snow'…might well be his reply." So it can be seen as a homage to Paxford when, in *The Silver Chair*, Lewis writes that Narnia was happy under King Rilian, but that Puddleglum "often pointed out that bright mornings brought on wet afternoons, and that you couldn't expect good times to last".

Reepicheep, the Mouse, embodies the romantic virtues of chivalry, honour and humility together with a passion for adventure. Several years after writing *The Chronicles*, Lewis wrote that, "*The Voyage of the* Dawn Treader [is about] the spiritual life, (especially in Reepicheep)." Only a foot or two tall, Reepicheep is nevertheless fearless, proud and at the front of every battle. He is the Chief Mouse, considered the bravest of all the Talking Beasts. Known for his great balancing skills in fights, when he loses his tail in *Prince Caspian* and thus loses his balance, he appeals to Aslan for a new one. His

primary motive for wanting a tail, however, appears to involve pride: He fears that others will make fun of him. Reepicheep inspires such loyalty that the other mice offer to cut off their own tails so people won't notice that their chief's tail is missing. Reepicheep's life of ser-

vice to the King and Aslan epitomizes the spiritual quest of an Arthurian-style knight. At the end of *The Voyage of the Dawn Treader*, it is Reepicheep who sails off alone in his small boat, seeking Aslan's country beyond the World's End. As he sets off, he tosses his sword into the water. His fighting days are over, but his greatest quest is just beginning.

Rilian is the son of King Caspian and Ramandu's daughter. When his mother is killed by a huge green serpent at the beginning of *The Silver Chair*, Prince Rilian sets off to find the snake and avenge her murder. Before his mother's death, Rilian was a charming and carefree young knight who loved to laugh and tell stories with his friends. But after her death, his search for the snake leaves him "tired and distraught", as one of the owls tells Eustace and Jill. Rilian is bewitched by a beautiful woman, who calls herself the Queen of Underland or the Lady of the Green Kirtle. She is able to transform herself into a deadly green snake. She enslaves the Prince in her underground kingdom, making him forget his former life on the surface. He only remembers his true identity for one hour a day, but the evil Queen keeps him strapped into a magical silver chair during that hour so he cannot escape. Once Rilian is rescued by Eustace, Jill and Puddleglum, he fights bravely to free them all from the wicked Witch and to avenge his mother's murder. He goes on to rule Narnia after his father's death. Fair and

The noble mouse Reepicheep (opposite, below), is one of the bravest of Narnia's creatures.

Roonwit, a loyal counsellor to King Tirian in The Last Battle, is a Centaur like this one (right, in a concept drawing for the movie The Lion, the Witch and the Wardrobe).

honest, Rilian "ruled Narnia well and the land was happy in his days.…"

In *The Last Battle*, **Roonwit** the Centaur warns King Tirian that disastrous times are coming. Like all Centaurs, he is able to read messages in the stars, and, contrary to rumours from the Calormenes, he knows that Aslan cannot be in Narnia. With a golden beard on his human face and a chestnut coat of horsehair on his flanks, Roonwit speaks the truth fearlessly in a booming voice to a king who is reluctant to hear it. Refusing to believe the false tale of Aslan's return, Roonwit says, "…I know there are liars on earth; there are none among the stars." It is a great loss to Tirian and Narnia when Roonwit is killed by a Calormene arrow on his way to help gather the Narnian army.

Shasta, who is really the missing **Prince Cor** of Archenland, is kept almost as if he were a slave by Arsheesh, a poor Calormene fisherman. Shasta learns at the beginning of *The Horse and His Boy* that Arsheesh is not his father. When he hears the fisherman planning to sell him to a Calormene lord, Shasta runs away with a horse named Bree, who turns out to be a proud Narnian talking warhorse. Distrustful of strangers, fearful of getting caught and generally feeling sorry for himself, Shasta grows and matures during his flight northward, eventually finding

"Now, Roonwit," said the King. "Do you bring us more news of Aslan?"

In The Last Battle, *King Tirian* (left) *fights a losing battle to save the old Narnia.*
In the movie The Lion, the Witch and the Wardrobe, *Tumnus the Faun* (opposite) *is the first Narnian to meet a child from Earth.*

courage to persevere, to trust others and to be more mindful of others' fears and problems. Shasta is entrusted with a life-and-death mission: to save Narnia and Archenland from the invading Calormene army. Accepting this grave responsibility, he puts Narnia's safety before his own. In doing so, he fulfils the prophecy of his birth. The boy is the twin of the fun-loving Prince Corin and the son of King Lune of Archenland. He takes his real name, Cor, and he becomes King after his father's death.

Tirian is "the last of the Kings of Narnia" because Narnia comes to an end during his reign. A mercurial figure whose emotions sometimes rage out of control, King Tirian is often rash and quick to anger, but he fights for what is right and is praised by Aslan near the end of *The Last Battle* as one "who stood firm at the darkest hour". Early in *The Last Battle*, Tirian understands that Narnia is in peril. He implores Aslan to help, but there is no apparent answer. So he summons the four children who rescued Narnia in past times of need, calling out, "Children! Children! Friends of Narnia! Quick. Come to me. Across the worlds I call you...."

Trumpkin, a Red Dwarf, is one of the most beloved creatures in Narnia. In *Prince Caspian* he is the first to greet the Pevensies when they arrive at the ancient ruins of Cair Paravel. He has a sceptical nature and harbours serious doubts about the children's royal past. But Trumpkin has been sent on this mission by his leader, Prince Caspian, who needs the help of Narnia's High Kings and Queens. Trumpkin's loyalty to the prince forces him to entertain the possibility that mere children might be of some help. When the children politely demonstrate that they are better fighters, better archers and more gifted healers than the Dwarf, he is persuaded by the facts. A realist through and through, Trumpkin is also brave and helpful and filled with good humour. The siblings embarrass him by nicknaming him DLF (Dear Little Friend). Trumpkin remains at Caspian's side throughout the three books in which the prince, later king, appears. In *The Voyage of the* Dawn Treader, Trumpkin is King Caspian's Lord Regent, and in *The Silver Chair*, although deaf with age by then, he is running the kingdom while the doddering old King Caspian is travelling. It is Trumpkin who orders the owl Glimfeather to take good care of Jill and Eustace.

Tumnus, a Faun who lives in the Lantern Waste, plays a crucial role in *The Chronicles*.

He is the beginning of Narnia in two ways: His image—a faun with an umbrella in a snowy wood—was the first picture from Narnia to come into C. S. Lewis's mind. And he is the first Narnian whom Lucy meets when she emerges from the wardrobe. An emotional creature who weeps openly in front of Lucy, Tumnus is a lover of comforts, keeping a tidy home in a snug cave. He loves

"Come to me. Across the worlds I call you...."

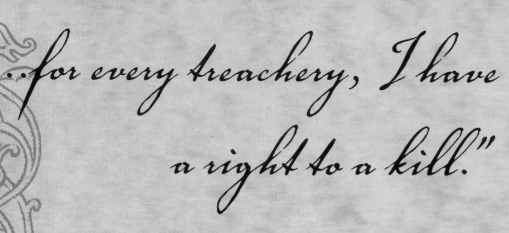

"...for every treachery, I have a right to a kill."

to read, judging from the books that line his shelves. He also loves company, keeping an extra chair "for a friend", treating Lucy to tea and chatting on and on with her. A talented musician, Tumnus plays his flute so beautifully that it makes Lucy "want to cry and laugh and dance and go to sleep all at the same time". His job, however, as he sadly admits, is to be a kidnapper for the evil White Witch. But Tumnus turns out to be a better friend than a kidnapper, refusing to hand Lucy over to the Witch or even to inform on her. The Witch turns him to stone for his act of defiance. Aslan breathes life back into Tumnus, who later becomes a good friend and trusted advisor to the Pevensie siblings when they become Kings and Queens of Narnia.

VILLAINS

"[B]efore the new, clean world I gave you is seven hours old, a force of evil has already entered it; waked and brought hither by this son of Adam." —Aslan, in *The Magician's Nephew*

That "force of evil"—the original and greatest evil in *The Chronicles*—is **Jadis**, later known as the **White Witch.** Jadis is seven feet tall and very beautiful, with skin as white as snow and bright red lips. She is physically strong and possesses magical powers. Many wild tales are told about the Witch. It is said, for example, that she can read men's minds, but she cannot. It also is said that she is half giant and half Jinn (a magical race similar to genies). But, in fact, she is the sole survivor of the Royal House of Charn, a nonhuman race who look like humans and once lived on the dead world of Charn. It was Jadis who wiped out her race in ancient times (long before the period in which *The Magician's Nephew* takes place) by speaking the Deplorable Word, a powerfully destructive magical incantation. After she speaks the Deplorable Word, Jadis falls into a deep, enchanted sleep until Digory, displaying a foolish lack of self-control, rings the magic bell of Charn and awakens her. Restored to life, she follows Digory and Polly to Earth and then to Narnia, where she introduces evil into the new world. She would have destroyed Narnia with her evil, just as she killed everyone on Charn, but Aslan forces her to retreat to the north. Almost a thousand years later, she comes back to Narnia, falsely calls herself Queen (although Narnians dub her the White Witch), and rules with fear for

Jadis, the White Witch (opposite, in the movie *The Lion, the Witch and the Wardrobe*), *is the epitome of evil in the first two books of* The Chronicles of Narnia.

one hundred years, imposing a century of winter on the world. In the midst of the long winter, Aslan, with the help of the Pevensies, brings her reign of evil to a close and restores freedom and the seasons to Narnia.

Like the Greek gorgon Medusa, the White Witch can turn people and beasts into stone. Lewis also credited another ancient character, Circe, as inspiration for the Witch. Circe tempted men with magical food and turned them into animals in *The Odyssey*; Jadis creates enchanted Turkish Delight and uses it to make Edmund do her will in *The Lion, the Witch and the Wardrobe*.

Jadis is the almost-invincible evil counterpart to Aslan's goodness. But she is far from alone when it comes to people and creatures who practise wickedness in *The Chronicles*.

Evil appears in every book of *The Chronicles* as a force against which Aslan and his supporters must contend. Lewis created a host of characters who populate the dark side of the Narnian world.

Merely Comical Creatures

Monopods, Duffers and Dufflepuds are three names for the same small, foolish dwarfs in *The Voyage of the Dawn Treader* who inhabit a well-tended island in the Great Eastern Ocean. They were turned into creatures with one huge leg and a mushroom-like foot after disobeying a magician named Coriakin. Transformed in this way, the Duffers can only hop around, although their feet *do* come in handy: They sleep under them to keep out the rain or sun. The Duffers hate their new appearance so much they turn themselves invisible—but then try to force Lucy Pevensie to reverse the spell. (Only a young girl can work the spell that controls the dwarfs' invisibility.) Lewis's invention of the Duffers may have been influenced by a medieval book called *The Bestiary*, which features skiapods—creatures that look like Duffers and sleep under their feet.

The Lady of the Green Kirtle, who also calls herself Queen of Underland or Queen of the Deep Realm, appears only in *The Silver Chair*. Many who know her refer to her as the Witch. She is very beautiful, with a lovely musical laugh. She has the power to make people forget their old lives and their identities along with their most deeply held beliefs. She can also transform herself into a deadly green serpent, which is how she murders the Queen of Narnia, King Caspian's wife and Prince Rilian's mother. The Witch later enchants Rilian, trapping him in Underland where she has control over all the peoples who live beneath Narnia's surface.

Maugrim, the large grey Wolf, is the head of the White Witch's secret police. It is his job to round up the Witch's enemies so she can turn them into stone. The Wolf chases Susan, forcing Peter to kill Maugrim with his new sword. In the first American edition of *The Lion, the Witch and the Wardrobe*, Maugrim's name was changed to Fenris Ulf. In Norse myth, Fenris or Fenrisulfr (literally, "Fenris wolf") was the name of a huge, supernatural wolf who threatened the god Odin. This change of name, and all the other changes made in the early American editions of *The Chronicles*, have been removed, and the books now appear the way Lewis originally wrote them.

Nikabrik is a Black Dwarf in *Prince Caspian* who has been made suspicious, hateful and untrustworthy by the prolonged suffering imposed on him and the other Old Narnians under the reign of Miraz. When Caspian is thrown from his horse while fleeing Miraz, Nikabrik is in the small band of Old Narnians who first finds the prince unconscious in the forest. "Kill it," Nikabrik advises his companions, referring to Caspian. "We can't let it live. It would betray us." The advice is typical of Nikabrik's nature. He doesn't believe in Aslan and thinks the White Witch's leadership was good for the Dwarfs. He is desperate to regain control of Narnia for the Dwarfs. So he turns against Aslan and argues in favour

The captain of the Witch's secret police, Maugrim (opposite) is a vicious, untiring predator in The Lion, the Witch and the Wardrobe. *Nikabrik (left), the suspicious and untrustworthy dwarf in* Prince Caspian, *is killed in the darkness.*

of an alliance with the White Witch. This precipitates a fight among Caspian's counsellors that draws supernatural attacks in total darkness from an evil female spirit and a Wer-Wolf. In the confused struggle, Nikabrik attacks the good badger Trufflehunter, and is killed in the darkness, although it is never revealed by whom.

Shift is an evil Ape responsible for bringing ruin upon Narnia in *The Last Battle*. In his quest for power, he forces the trusting donkey Puzzle to drape a lion's skin over his body to create the illusion that Aslan has returned. Since Aslan hasn't been seen in Narnia for hundreds of years, Narnians don't know what he looks like and are easily fooled. Puzzle isn't evil but he doesn't know what to believe, so he allows himself to be used by Shift. Living up to his name, Shift is manipulative, sneaky and dishonest. He conspires with the evil Calormenes to overthrow the King of Narnia. Shift's plan works but, ultimately, the demon Tash—who Shift thought to be a comrade—carries him off.

Aslan knows that deep down, Puzzle's heart is pure, and he is allowed to join the rest of the friends of Narnia in the real Narnia.

Tash is the demon god of Calormen. The bloodthirsty, cruel being—called "Tash the inexorable, the irresistible"—has the torso of a man, four arms, talons in place of fingernails and the head of a bird of prey. When the Calormenes finally see Tash for the first time, they are terrified. At the end of *The Last Battle*, the villain god is banished by Peter.

The Tisroc is the hereditary name of the ruler of Calormen, a desert country far to the south of Narnia. In *The Horse and His Boy*, the Tisroc is cruel, killing people at the least provocation. He abhors the fact that he has no control over Narnia, and sends his son Rabadash to conquer Archenland, the country between Calormen and Narnia, so that Narnia will be more open to invasion. Rabadash fails in his mission, although further generations take up his warlike ways.

The newest retelling of The Chronicles of Narnia *is the movie* The Lion, the Witch and the Wardrobe. *In one scene* (below), *Peter, Lucy and Susan tend to Edmund.*

Two more characters from the movie (opposite) *are the White Witch, played by Tilda Swinton, and a Dwarf, played by actor Kiran Shah.*

7 May 1954

Dear Joan,

As for doing more Narnian books than 7, isn't it better to stop when people are still asking for more than to go on till they are tired?

Love from,
yours,

C.S. Lewis

The Story Continues

C. S. Lewis's worldwide fame was confirmed in Autumn 1947, when Time, America's leading news weekly, put the writer's picture on its cover. Time was celebrating the popularity of The Screwtape Letters, Lewis's best-selling book of imagined letters from a senior functionary in the devil's byzantine bureaucracy. Still, Lewis was convinced that his literary fame would die long before he did.

Writing to a friend in 1951, Lewis suggested that he was destined to be "one of those men who *was* a famous writer in his forties and dies unknown". Now, however, more than half a century since the publication of *The Lion, the Witch and the Wardrobe* and more than forty years after his own death, Lewis's immense readership and reputation continue to grow.

Although C. S. Lewis wrote dozens of books on literature and religion, two hundred essays and almost eighty poems, it was his seven books for children that brought him his widest audience. The books were greeted with critical praise and sizeable sales from the start, and both the praise and the sales have only multiplied with the years. Once the series was published, Lewis routinely had to devote an hour before dawn every morning to answering the letters that flooded his letterbox from children all around the world. The children asked questions or shared their thoughts about Narnia with the man who had led them out of their own lives and through a magic wardrobe. Perhaps unsurprisingly, given the eternal vitality of Lewis's voice on the page, the volume of letters barely slowed after his death. It wasn't that the children did not know he had died. Rather it seemed that the mere fact of his passing was nothing that could or should prevent communication with such a man. One little boy even wrote to Lewis, saying he was sorry to hear that Lewis had died.

Today, confirming the feelings of the children who still correspond with *The Chronicles'* creator, Lewis lives on. There are more than eighty-five million copies of *The Chronicles of Narnia* in print in almost thirty languages. At least four famous illustrators, beginning with Pauline Baynes, have interpreted the stories in differing ways through their art. Now a new generation of artists, actors and special effects

Unofficial Illustrators

Many of the children who wrote to Lewis were so involved in the stories that they sent art they had created based on the characters. Lewis was very appreciative of these gifts and always responded with sincerity and warmth.

28th. April 1954
Dear Hugh,
Oh, very good. Eustace as a dragon is your best picture yet. Really awesome! Love to all.
Yours,
C. S. Lewis

[24 January 1954]
...[The] picture of the Prince and Jill and the Chair [is] very good—especially the Prince's legs, for legs aren't too easy to draw, are they? Noelie's White Witch is superb!—just as proud and wicked as I meant her to be....
yours ever
C. S. Lewis

[30 January 1954]
Dear Hila,
Upon my word, a statue of Reepicheep. He stares at me from my mantelpiece with just the right mixture of courtesy and readiness to fight....
yours ever
C. S. Lewis

The Minotaur (opposite), Lucy (above) and Peter, facing danger with his sisters (right), are all images from the Disney-Walden Media movie The Lion, the Witch and the Wardrobe.

A Picture Is Worth a Thousand Words: Pauline Baynes

"[Lewis] was, to me, the most kindly and tolerant of authors.…As I remember, he only once asked for an alteration—and then with many apologies—when I (with my little knowledge) had drawn one of the characters rowing a boat facing the wrong direction!"

For readers worldwide, the drawings and watercolours of Narnia and its inhabitants are inseparable from Lewis's words. Narnia has been interpreted over the decades by a number of well-known illustrators, including Chris Van Allsburg, the writer and artist who created *The Polar Express*. But the images that define Narnia were produced by the books' original illustrator, the previously little-known Pauline Baynes, who worked closely with Lewis himself to produce the first visuals of the Narnian world.

Baynes drew approximately 350 illustrations in pen and ink over a period of five years. Nearly fifty years later, she coloured them in with watercolors for a new edition marking the one-hundred-year anniversary of Lewis's birth.

Baynes lived in India until she was five years old, and then attended private schools in England. After art school, she became an art teacher. Then she began illustrating children's books, including several that she had written herself. Lewis told Baynes that he contacted her after asking a shop clerk for the name of an illustrator who drew animals and children very well. The clerk recommended Baynes. But Lewis also had admired Baynes's work in one of Tolkien's early books, *Farmer Giles of Ham*.

Lewis gave Baynes a few sketches of his own to work from—one of the Monopods from *The Voyage of the Dawn Treader* and a map for *Prince Caspian*. He preferred her to use her own imagination. In 1956, *The Last Battle* won the Carnegie Medal as the best children's book of the year. Baynes wrote to congratulate Lewis and he replied, "Is it not rather 'our' Medal?"

Surprisingly, the two only met in person twice. Baynes, who was only in her mid-twenties when she first started working with Lewis, recalls one awkward lunch at Oxford with him and a group of his friends and one meeting in London. Lewis, she said, was nervous around her; he once told his friend George Sayer, "Pauline is far too pretty."

Even though she illustrated more than one hundred children's books, Baynes will forever be known as the woman who drew Narnia. "I think it's the fate of the illustrator," she says. "Look at Ernest Shepard. He was so brilliant and did so much fine work, but people only associate him with Pooh and Piglet, and Toad of Toad Hall. It's the penalty of hitching your wagon to a star."

technicians are about to retell Lewis's stories in a series of major motion pictures which are certain to capture a global audience, much like *The Lord of the Rings*, the movie trilogy based on the books by Lewis's friend and contemporary J. R. R. Tolkien.

The Chronicles of Narnia, in short, are a worldwide, multimedia phenomenon.

Throughout his life, Lewis displayed a talent for seeing the wonder in ordinary things. He was moved to joy by the simple objects of nature; he could see greatness in a child's scrawled drawing. While he routinely made the ordinary seem extraordinary, he also possessed the corollary ability to see the ordinariness in extraordinary happenings. Lewis could make it seem that miracles and magical feats are daily occurrences. These talents may help explain Narnia's continuing appeal to its readers.

Chad Walsh, reviewing *Prince Caspian* in *The New York Times Book Review* of November 11, 1951, was struck by just this talent of Lewis's. "The story is for boys and girls who like their dwarfs and fauns as solid as the traffic policeman on the corner," he wrote, focusing on Lewis's ability to portray the fantastic with everyday solidity.

In 1998, the world celebrated what would have been Lewis's hundredth birthday. HarperCollins, the publisher of *The Chronicles of Narnia*, brought out new editions of the books, including a set with newly coloured illustrations by Pauline Baynes, the original illustrator. In London, a twelve-year-old schoolgirl won a national competition by creating a greetings card based on *The Chronicles of Narnia*. The competition, which benefited a national children's charity, was sponsored by Microsoft. The winning card was just one small part of an exhibit about

Susan, her face hidden in Aslan's mane, and Lucy weep for the Great Lion after his death on the Stone Table in this moving scene from The Lion, the Witch and the Wardrobe.

"Dear Lucy... some day you will be old enough to start reading fairy tales again. ..."

Narnia and the life of its author at the London Toy and Model Museum. The Royal Shakespeare Company performed a stage adaptation of *The Lion, the Witch and the Wardrobe* in Stratford-upon-Avon. The Royal Mail issued a series of postage stamps called "Magical Worlds" to honour England's greatest fantasy writers. In this series was a twenty-six-pence stamp featuring Lucy, Mr Tumnus and Aslan.

Many of the current generation of fantasy writers acknowledge their debt to *The Chronicles*. J. K. Rowling, the author of the Harry Potter books, says the Narnia stories were among her favourites as a child and she lists C. S. Lewis as one of three authors who were her biggest inspiration. Another best-selling children's fantasy writer, Eoin Colfer, the Irish author of the Artemis Fowl books, says *Prince Caspian* was his introduction to the world of fantasy and was the book that made the biggest impression on him.

Over the years, many children wrote to Lewis asking if there would be any more Narnia books. "And why not write stories for yourself to fill up the gaps in Narnian history?" he suggested in response. "I've left you plenty of hints—especially where Lucy and the Unicorn are talking in *The Last Battle*. I feel *I* have done all I can!" Today, in the age of

The White Witch questions the imprisoned Edmund (left) in this shot from the Disney-Walden Media movie The Lion, the Witch and the Wardrobe.

Susan (opposite) *pauses with danger close by in this scene from the movie* The Lion, the Witch and the Wardrobe.

the Internet, hundreds of children and adults have taken him up on his suggestion. Numerous web sites are filled with fan fiction based on *The Chronicles*. Narnia lovers from around the world post original short stories, poems, recipes and artwork based on the seven books. The Internet also has spawned hundreds of web sites discussing different aspects of the tales—from themes and favourite characters, to Lewis's life and the geography of the Narnian countryside, complete with quizzes, trivia questions and historical events and writings that might have inspired Lewis.

The newest topic of discussion and debate is the movie from Walt Disney Pictures and Walden Media that is based on *The Lion, the Witch and the Wardrobe*. Web sites have tracked the film's every move, from conception to casting and production on locations throughout New Zealand. Walden Media owns the rights to film all seven books, and chose to begin with *The Lion, the Witch and the Wardrobe* because it was the first book published and the best known. The director, Andrew Adamson, is a visual-effects genius whose best work, including the animated hits *Shrek* and *Shrek 2*, has involved stories that are ostensibly for children but appeal to all ages. Utilizing Adamson's background in special effects, the movie combines live action with computer-generated animation and animatronics (robotlike puppets to portray certain aspects of characters). This combination of techniques represents the most technically ambitious motion picture project ever undertaken, according to the filmmakers. With Douglas Gresham, Lewis's stepson, as co-producer, the films also are assured of remaining true to the books' vision.

The Walden Media productions mark the first time Hollywood has focused major

budgets and modern special effects on the technically challenging task of bringing Narnia to the screen. But *The Chronicles* have been dramatised before with varying degrees of success. In the past few decades, five made-for-television versions were produced in England. The first, in 1967, was a black-and-white adaptation of *The Lion, the Witch and the Wardrobe*; an animated movie version followed in 1979. In the 1980s, the BBC aired live-action series of *The Lion, the Witch and the Wardrobe* and *The Silver Chair*, along with a production that combined the stories of *Prince Caspian* and *The Voyage of the* Dawn Treader. Anticipating the BBC productions, Walter Cronkite, the revered CBS newscaster, predicted on television in 1979: "*The Chronicles of Narnia* have genuine family appeal. In a dramatic and compelling way these classics present human values often lacking in today's television: loyalty, courage, caring, responsibility, truthfulness and compassion."

Evidence of the ongoing life of *The Chronicles of Narnia* ranges from the trivial to the

...the movie combines live action with computer-generated animation and animatronics...

126

Peter (opposite) *prepares to ride into battle in the movie* The Lion, the Witch and the Wardrobe.

More movie images: The White Witch (left) *steps out of her sledge, and Mr Tumnus the Faun plays the pipes.*

profound. On the trivial side, there are numerous products based on *The Chronicles*, including four different board games, three computer-based video games and a puzzle. An Advent calendar, cookbooks, wall calendars, trivia books, journals and maps are among the many other Narnia products.

On the more profound side of Lewis's legacy, The C. S. Lewis Foundation was officially created in 1986. One of its main goals was to restore Lewis's longtime home, The Kilns, to its authentic 1940s appearance. With the help of charitable donations and many volunteers from England and America, the house was repainted, refurnished, landscaped and repaired. The Kilns is now used as a residence for graduate students from Oxford and as a study centre for those interested in Lewis's entire body of work, including his considerable writings on Christianity. The C. S. Lewis Study Centre at The Kilns focuses on the study of Christian thought and art.

Lewis dedicated *The Lion, the Witch and the Wardrobe*, the first book he wrote in the series, to his young goddaughter, Lucy Barfield.

His loving dedication to the real-life Lucy now sounds somewhat like a prophecy:

My Dear Lucy,

I wrote this story for you, but when I began it I had not realized that girls grow quicker than books. As a result you are already too old for fairy tales, and by the time it is printed and bound you will be older still. But some day you will be old enough to start reading fairy tales again. You can then take it down from some upper shelf, dust it, and tell me what you think of it. I shall probably be too deaf to hear, and too old to understand, a word you say, but I shall still be

your affectionate Godfather,

C. S. Lewis

As the decades pass, Lewis's prediction has proven true as *The Chronicles of Narnia* continue to engage generations of readers, young and old. At the end of *The Last Battle*, Aslan calls to the inhabitants of Narnia to go ever deeper into the new world, to "Come further in! Come further up!" And so it goes that millions of inhabitants of Earth continue to follow Aslan's call into Narnia, becoming part of a world that leaves them better for having visited.

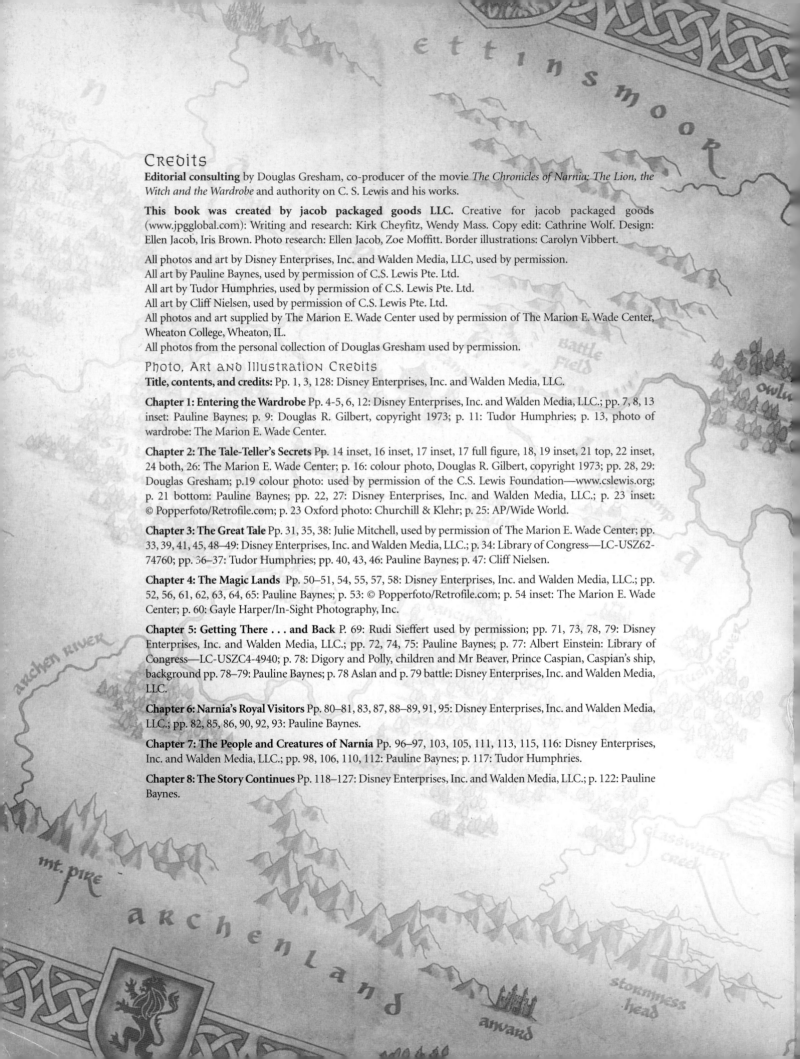

CREDITS

Editorial consulting by Douglas Gresham, co-producer of the movie *The Chronicles of Narnia: The Lion, the Witch and the Wardrobe* and authority on C. S. Lewis and his works.

This book was created by jacob packaged goods LLC. Creative for jacob packaged goods (www.jpgglobal.com): Writing and research: Kirk Cheyfitz, Wendy Mass. Copy edit: Cathrine Wolf. Design: Ellen Jacob, Iris Brown. Photo research: Ellen Jacob, Zoe Moffitt. Border illustrations: Carolyn Vibbert.

All photos and art by Disney Enterprises, Inc. and Walden Media, LLC, used by permission.
All art by Pauline Baynes, used by permission of C.S. Lewis Pte. Ltd.
All art by Tudor Humphries, used by permission of C.S. Lewis Pte. Ltd.
All art by Cliff Nielsen, used by permission of C.S. Lewis Pte. Ltd.
All photos and art supplied by The Marion E. Wade Center used by permission of The Marion E. Wade Center, Wheaton College, Wheaton, IL.
All photos from the personal collection of Douglas Gresham used by permission.

Photo, Art and Illustration Credits

Title, contents, and credits: Pp. 1, 3, 128: Disney Enterprises, Inc. and Walden Media, LLC.

Chapter 1: Entering the Wardrobe Pp. 4-5, 6, 12: Disney Enterprises, Inc. and Walden Media, LLC.; pp. 7, 8, 13 inset: Pauline Baynes; p. 9: Douglas R. Gilbert, copyright 1973; p. 11: Tudor Humphries; p. 13, photo of wardrobe: The Marion E. Wade Center.

Chapter 2: The Tale-Teller's Secrets Pp. 14 inset, 16 inset, 17 inset, 17 full figure, 18, 19 inset, 21 top, 22 inset, 24 both, 26: The Marion E. Wade Center; p. 16: colour photo, Douglas R. Gilbert, copyright 1973; pp. 28, 29: Douglas Gresham; p.19 colour photo: used by permission of the C.S. Lewis Foundation—www.cslewis.org; p. 21 bottom: Pauline Baynes; pp. 22, 27: Disney Enterprises, Inc. and Walden Media, LLC.; p. 23 inset: © Popperfoto/Retrofile.com; p. 23 Oxford photo: Churchill & Klehr; p. 25: AP/Wide World.

Chapter 3: The Great Tale Pp. 31, 35, 38: Julie Mitchell, used by permission of The Marion E. Wade Center; pp. 33, 39, 41, 45, 48–49: Disney Enterprises, Inc. and Walden Media, LLC.; p. 34: Library of Congress—LC-USZ62-74760; pp. 36–37: Tudor Humphries; pp. 40, 43, 46: Pauline Baynes; p. 47: Cliff Nielsen.

Chapter 4: The Magic Lands Pp. 50–51, 54, 55, 57, 58: Disney Enterprises, Inc. and Walden Media, LLC.; pp. 52, 56, 61, 62, 63, 64, 65: Pauline Baynes; p. 53: © Popperfoto/Retrofile.com; p. 54 inset: The Marion E. Wade Center; p. 60: Gayle Harper/In-Sight Photography, Inc.

Chapter 5: Getting There . . . and Back P. 69: Rudi Sieffert used by permission; pp. 71, 73, 78, 79: Disney Enterprises, Inc. and Walden Media, LLC.; pp. 72, 74, 75: Pauline Baynes; p. 77: Albert Einstein: Library of Congress—LC-USZC4-4940; p. 78: Digory and Polly, children and Mr Beaver, Prince Caspian, Caspian's ship, background pp. 78–79: Pauline Baynes; p. 78 Aslan and p. 79 battle: Disney Enterprises, Inc. and Walden Media, LLC.

Chapter 6: Narnia's Royal Visitors Pp. 80–81, 83, 87, 88–89, 91, 95: Disney Enterprises, Inc. and Walden Media, LLC.; pp. 82, 85, 86, 90, 92, 93: Pauline Baynes.

Chapter 7: The People and Creatures of Narnia Pp. 96–97, 103, 105, 111, 113, 115, 116: Disney Enterprises, Inc. and Walden Media, LLC.; pp. 98, 106, 110, 112: Pauline Baynes; p. 117: Tudor Humphries.

Chapter 8: The Story Continues Pp. 118–127: Disney Enterprises, Inc. and Walden Media, LLC.; p. 122: Pauline Baynes.